Five-Minute Lessons in Successful Selling

Rodney Young

FIVE-MINUTE LESSONS IN SUCCESSFUL SELLING

Increase Your Sales Skills
Without Going Back to School

A SPECTRUM BOOK

Prentice-Hall, Inc., Englewood Cliffs, New Jersey 07632

Library of Congress Cataloging in Publication Data

Young, Rodney.
   Five-minute lessons in successful selling.

   "A Spectrum Book."
   Includes index.
   1. Selling.   I. Title.
HF5438.25.Y69   1985   658.8'5   84-24760
ISBN 0-13-321670-5
ISBN 0-13-321662-4 (pbk.)

1   2   3   4   5   6   7   8   9   10

ISBN 0-13-321670-5

ISBN 0-13-321662-4 {PBK.}

Editorial/production supervision
and book design by Marilyn E. Beckford
Cover design © 1985 by Jeannette Jacobs
Manufacturing buyer: Frank Grieco

This book is available at a special discount when ordered in
bulk quantities. Contact Prentice-Hall, Inc., General
Publishing Division, Special Sales, Englewood Cliffs, N.J. 07632.

Prentice-Hall International (UK) Limited, *London*
Prentice-Hall of Australia Pty. Limited, *Sydney*
Prentice-Hall Canada Inc., *Toronto*
Prentice-Hall Hispanoamericana, S.A., *Mexico*
Prentice-Hall of India Private Limited, *New Delhi*
Prentice-Hall of Japan, Inc., *Tokyo*
Prentice-Hall of Southeast Asia Pte. Ltd., *Singapore*
Whitehall Books Limited, *Wellington, New Zealand*
Editora Prentice-Hall do Brasil Ltda., *Rio de Janeiro*

To Bonnie

she believed

Contents

Preface

It will take you less than five minutes to read this preface. It is my guess that you have bought this book not only because you are interested in sharpening your selling skills but also because you feel the need to do so in a hurry. Each of these one hundred five-minute lessons is about some key aspect of selling, and so you may finish a lesson wishing that it were longer and feeling that you would like to know more about the topic of the lesson. It is my fervent hope that this happens often as you read the book.

However this might be, the average time that most adults are willing (or able) to attend to one subject is limited to about eight minutes. The five minutes or so required to read each lesson assures that it will get your full attention. Thus, giving it your undivided concentration for this brief period helps to assure that you will *learn* the lesson and see far quicker results where results count: in your commission check.

You may have read several or many books on selling before coming to *Five-Minute Lessons in Successful Selling*. Most of those books have covered the basics of selling: getting attention, arousing interest, creating desire, impelling action. This book, too, is organized around those important concepts. There are, however, some striking differences—differences that will make reading it a unique experience. Of course, every writer of books on selling brings his or her sales personality to the work produced, and this book is no exception to that rule. Yet, my work as a business journalist has given me the opportunity to interview and learn from scores of working sales professionals, each with a different approach to certain selling problems, and each having innovative *solutions* to those problems. I have chronicled some of these selling strategies in feature articles for the *Houston Business Journal*, for Prentice-Hall's Bureau of Business Practice, for *Specialty Salesman* and *Selling Direct*, for Dartnel, and for other publishers, but you will find here techniques and methods that are practiced by master salespeople, but that, to my knowledge, are not yet part of the common fund of selling knowledge as it appears in print.

In this regard you will study with special interest the lessons on dressing, the lesson on "metaclothing," the lesson called "The Truth About Positive Thinking," the lesson on relaxation through meditation, the information on state-of-the-art selling devices, and the information concerning selling and the right half of the brain. The research on what it takes to make a selling pro and the discussion on habit formation will be of special interest to you if you aspire to the title of "sales professional."

Could it be said that this is the only book on selling you will ever need? I hope not. The inspiration you will need to attain a high level of motivation must constantly be fed by fresh ideas—ideas that will be new to you, regardless of how long ago they were "discovered" by others. Some lessons in this book are primarily "inspirational" rather than purely instructional. You will want to read these lessons again and again. Such a lesson is the first lesson in the book, "The Seven Deadly Sins of Selling," and so is the last lesson—"Seven Keys to Harmony and Happiness in Business Relationships."

Although I have said that the first and last lessons are primarily inspirational, let me qualify that in an important manner. If you will so thoroughly *learn these two lessons* that they become a part of your consciousness—so thoroughly that they are imbedded in your very nervous system—*you will know everything else of substance in the book*!

1

The Customer
Comes Last

The heresy implied in the title of this chapter is more apparent than real. There are some things that the sales representative should learn to do well before coming face to face with a customer, however. This chapter examines some of the most important of these things.

Although it is certainly possible to overdo the business of preparation (I had a relative who spent so long getting ready to repair a roof that he nearly lost the contents of his house to a rainstorm), it is also possible to move too quickly. Experience is a good teacher, but the school of experience carries an exorbitant fee for its training courses. Perhaps just a little extra time learning how to start can save money, time, and energy in the long run.

Notice that I said *learning* how to start—not *reading* how to start. This a distinction that you will find important. When you were in school, you understood well the difference between *understanding* a subject and *remembering* it. Please remember this distinction now. Memorize at least the central idea of each lesson, embodied in each of the headings and in the various italicized passages. Memorization convinces those subconscious portions of the mind of the importance of the material; it stores the material for easier recall in a way that just plain reading cannot do. Try it both ways; you'll see what I mean.

LESSON NO. 1:
THE SEVEN DEADLY SINS OF SELLING

High on your list of first things should be taking positive steps toward eradicating these seven deadly sins. Certainly there are other sins; perhaps there are some as bad as these, maybe even worse. But these sins (bad habits, actually) are perhaps more common than others. Memorize them and begin at once to uproot each one from your consciousness:

1. Fear
2. Procrastination
3. Forgetfulness
4. Verbosity
5. Dishonesty
6. Familiarity
7. Laziness

This five-minute lesson will examine each one of these sins to help you impress upon your mind the necessity for taking positive corrective action.

1. *Fear.* Countless thousands of sales are lost every day simply because salespeople are afraid to ask for the order, afraid to ask for a large order, afraid to ask for action *now*— instead of "next week," "after the first," "next trip,"—even afraid to call on customers. As a famous statesman once said, "We have nothing to fear but fear itself."

2. *Procrastination.* Putting things off is the surest way to see that they will never get done. You may convince yourself that you have more to do than there is time for you to do it in. To kill this deadly sin before it destroys you, get into the list-making habit. Start each day by making a list of things you have to do that day. Then add one more item for your "*do* jar." At the end of the day, if you have anything left, undone on your list of items, add each item which has been undone for more than three days to the "*do* jar." The next day, pull a slip of paper at random from your "*do* jar," and make that the *first thing you do that day*. Then proceed with doing the other items on your list. This system will prevent you from continually shoving unpleasant tasks to the bottom of the list, where they will eventually be forgotten.

3. *Forgetfulness.* Proper record keeping is an aid to memory. You may think that you are "too busy" to write things down, but the truth is that you are too busy to spend precious minutes wracking your brain for facts and figures that you should have at your finger tips. Carry a small notebook in your shirt pocket or purse. Form the habit of writing just a twenty-word sentence in this notebook *after each call you make*. Begin the sentence with the name of your prospect, together with his or her company affiliation. Add just a couple of words to help you pigeon-hole pertinent details in your memory. Work hard at making sure you never forget the name of a client.

4. *Verbosity.* There is no question that you should thoroughly know the details of your proposition. You should likewise be ready to expound on any point about which your prospect expresses interest. However, "fast talkers" often kill more sales than they make, and this for the simple reason that people don't want to be *sold*; they would much rather feel that they have *bought*. This feeling can best be induced not by talking but by listening. There is a simple way of avoiding this deadly sin: Follow each presentation of features and benefits with a question. And keep your questions open-ended, to encourage meaningful answers. Ask questions that can't be answered by a simple "yes" or "no."

5. *Dishonesty.* It goes without saying (or does it?) that salespeople should never lie to their prospects and clients. Probably you would never tell a deliberate falsehood to your customer. But what about exaggeration? What about the calculated suppression of the disadvantages of your proposition? It is a sad commentary on the state of business ethics that most regulatory agencies consider much exaggeration to be "legitimate product puffery!" How would *you* feel if your client "exaggerated" the value of a check he gave you?

6. *Familiarity.* Some salespeople confuse familiarity with friendliness. Use a prospect's first name if it is obvious that he or she wishes to be on a first name basis. But you can never go wrong in using titles of respect—Mr., Mrs., Ms.—until you are sure that the prospect will not be offended. Don't assume it's okay to smoke. Don't pick up things on the prospect's desk. Don't put anything of yours on the desk without asking permission.

7. *Laziness.* It makes no difference how well you can make a presentation, answer objections, or close sales: If you won't make the necessary number of calls, you will fail. How many calls should you make in a day? That depends. How many calls *can* you make? You know the number you can make. Write that number down. Now add one to it. *That's how many calls you should try to make!*

LESSON NO. 2: GETTING PAST
THE KEEPER OF THE GATE

The "Guard" Is Not Your Enemy

If you have tended to think that the receptionist, or the secretary, or some other "guard" is your adversary, get over that notion. If you have a natural inclination to cleverness here, forget it. Forget such ploys as pretending that your call is personal. She or he has probably heard it all before.

Learn the guard's name. Cold calls work well with small

companies, but most large companies require that you make appointments through these buffers. Take the time to learn not only the client's name but the names of all those people who stand (or sit) between you and your prospect. *Always call the guard by name.* A good opening is one that uses the guard's name and includes a benefit that your product or service will confer: "Miss Hobart, I'm Jim Brown with Protecto. I have something new that will almost eliminate your company's credit losses. May I talk to Mr. Smith about this?"

Sell the Guard

Save your complete presentation for the person who can buy, but don't be coy with the buyer's secretary. Don't be afraid to tell this individual everything needed to convince him or her that what you are selling is important to the boss. The only real difference between the sale you hope to make and this "sale before the sale" is that the close will consist of getting the secretary to say "yes" to an appointment instead of "yes" to an outlay of funds for your product or service. The psychology involved is basically the same; you must get someone's *attention,* arouse his or her *interest,* and *convince* him or her that your product has enough value to merit an appointment. There must be enough emotional appeal to make the secretary desire to cooperate with you, and you must close by securing action on his or her part—he or she must pick up the phone and talk to the boss about you.

Use the Two-Call System

There are several methods for learning the names of the people at the top—the names of those who make the firm's important decisions. Various directories and other printed guides are available to you for this purpose. Learning the names of receptionists and executive secretaries takes a little more work. A very effective method of doing this is through the use of an *on-site-call conducted only for this purpose.* Set aside a day for the purpose of making, say, a dozen such calls. Don't try to sell anything on this day. Don't try for an appointment. Instead, your conversation will be directed toward "finding out if we can be of service." Ask the receptionist's name, give your name. Learn the name of the person who makes those important appointments as well as the one who makes the buying decisions. Write everything down for your next call. When you return, you will be prepared. This kind of call shouldn't take more than five or ten minutes.

Write a Message on Your Card

Assuming that you have convinced the receptionist or secretary that you should see the boss, there still may be the matter of her having the authority to make the actual appointment. Try this: Turn your card over, and write a message to the boss on the back of the card. The message can be something like "May I talk to you for five minutes about a program that can drastically cut your credit losses?" This brief message (or one like it) carried into the inner sanctum will sometimes get you an audience when nothing else will.

Try the Telephone

Sometimes you can't get through to see the buyer face to face without first getting through by telephone. Keep a list of your failures, those instances in which you couldn't get through to see the buyer in person. Let a few days go by and try again, this time by telephone.

LESSON NO. 3:
TIPS ON EFFECTIVE PROSPECTING

Determine Your Markets

Before you ever set foot out of your office, be absolutely sure that you know *who* your prospects are. It is important that you have much more than a general idea about what constitutes a prospect for your product or service. An aid to determining this is the *pre call profile*. Take the time to write out a concise description of the kind of person or organization that would likely use your product.

Survey Your Territory

Once you know *who* your prospects are, determine *where* they are. City directories, telephone books, and the like are helpful if your prospect profile suggests that your product has a limited appeal. However, if what you sell could be used by a mass market, a physical survey of the territory might be more useful. For example, if you sell boilers you would be limited to certain industrial prospects—the Yellow Pages would probably tell you where your prospects are located and do so more efficiently than driving all over the city would. On the other hand, a visual survey would show you where the strip shopping centers are located.

Set Up a Prospect Record System

One effective prospect file system consists of two file cards for each prospect; one card is filed alphabetically, and the other geographically. The rotary file systems (such as Rolodex) are ideal for this purpose. The cards are thin enough so that you can use carbon paper to make duplicate cards, yet heavy enough to stand extended use. Cards of about three by five inches should be adequate for your needs.

The Two Kinds of Prospects

There are two kinds of prospects. First there is the prospect who recognizes a need for what you are selling and is probably buying something similar from another supplier. Then there is the prospect who is either not aware of a need for your product or service or who is aware of a need but hasn't been motivated strongly enough to buy it. You must determine at the outset to which category your prospect belongs, and you should plot your selling strategy accordingly.

Ask Questions, but Don't
Give Prospects the Third Degree

Remember that prospects are not motivated to give you any information if they don't know you. Attempting to secure information without offering some is usually counterproductive. The printing rep who opens with the question "Who does your printing?" shouldn't be surprised to get the answer "That's none of your business." The same thing may happen if you ask for somebody's name without furnishing your own. Prospects who resent a question such as "How long have you been in business?" may soften when you reciprocate by volunteering such information as "I've been selling for this company for two years," or "I've been at it for ten years." *Another important point: try to give a reason for each question you ask of a prospect.* ("Miss Johnson, so that we can see if we can save you money, would you mind telling me what you pay for this item?")

**Don't Try to Sell Anything
While Prospecting**

Although there is much to be said for cold-call, one-shot selling where applicable, it is best to keep this separate from the prospecting function. This enables you to concentrate on your more limited (but equally important) objective and to be sure that you will do all the important things properly. There may still be days when you will want to go out and make cold calls *strictly for the purpose of selling on the spot.* Both the kind of product as well as the peculiar character of the territory you are working will influence your choice in this matter. But decide *first* what your objective is and *stick* to it!

LESSON NO. 4: DRESSING UP
AND DRESSING DOWN

Can You Be Overdressed?

A new salesperson is more often than not cautioned to be well dressed. Good advice, but what exactly does that mean? Should a man always wear a suit, or is a sport coat sometimes acceptable? How should a woman dress? May she ever wear just a skirt and blouse? Slacks? If you work on somebody's payroll, you may not have a choice—your employer may prefer that you follow a certain company policy. But if you're an independent, the issue may be important to you.

A Lesson from "Silent Cal"

Politicians know the value of identification. And people usually place greater credibility in the statements of those with whom they feel a sense of sameness. *Your clients and prospects need to feel this sameness with you.* President Calvin Coolidge understood the need of his "clients," the voters of the United States in the 1920s. Never one to indulge in superfluous talk, Coolidge conveyed his empathy for the small independent farmer by permitting himself to be photographed in a rural setting, dressed in bib overalls.

A Nod to the Brothers Smith

You will read in some books on selling that (for a man) being well-groomed means shaving at least once and sometimes twice a day. Again, it is necessary to remember the all-important fact that *the standards ap-*

plied by your customers are more valid than those of an arbitrary authority. For the most part, it is likely that customers prefer that salesmen do not have beards. However, there is a motorcycle shop in Houston in which all the salespeople wear black leather jackets or vests, and full beards!

Does Your Prospect Dress "Up" or "Down"?

If you have done a careful prospecting job before you make an actual sales call, you will know what is the proper attire for any particular sales call. Remember that some prospective customers prefer you to dress up; others are more comfortable dressing casually and feel better if you dress in the same manner. Don't try to guess which you should do—make determining this bit of information part of your precall fact-finding tour.

Play It Safe on the First Call

Although it is true that some of your clients will always dress casually and will prefer to see you dress that way, too, you should play it safe on the first call. Dress your best. Make the proper notes in your prospect records so that you will know what to do on your next visit. Just remember that nobody is going to be offended if you are dressed better than you have to be.

Buy the Best, or Buy Often

There is no question about it: *Good clothes look like good clothes*. They retain that look of newness far longer than do cheap clothes. But manufacturers of inexpensive clothing have worked some real miracles in recent years. You don't have to spend a fortune to buy good-looking clothing, but be prepared to replace things more often if you decide on a cheaper wardrobe.

New Shoes, New Shirt—Always

No matter how formally or how casually you dress, there are two articles of clothing that broadcast the kind of success (or failure) you have experienced. *Never wear a shirt or a blouse that isn't immaculate or one that doesn't look new!* Shoes should look that way, too. Prospects may judge you (perhaps unfairly) by the appearance of these two articles of clothing alone.

LESSON NO. 5: DRESSING UP
AND THE "METACLOTHING"

Making a good appearance involves much more than wearing clothes that look nice. As important as it is to be well dressed, there are several other things that you must be constantly aware of; things that your friends should tell you about but rarely do.

The "Jewelry" in Your Mouth

You could wear diamond rings on your fingers, a gold watch on your wrist, or a necklace of genuine South Sea Island pearls—and still fail to make a favorable impression.

Salespeople need to capitalize on their "pearly whites" just as their counterparts on television do. This is not to say that you should walk around looking like a Cheshire cat, with a phony, toothy smile etched into your face. But you can learn to smile and talk at the same time, so that even your voice has a smile in it. And you can be absolutely sure that your teeth are as nearly perfect as your dentist can make them. Good dental work doesn't come cheap, but neither does a nice car, nor any of the other things that you "wear" when you are well dressed.

Avoid "Eyeglass Contact"

The passage of anti–age discrimination laws has done virtually nothing to eliminate certain built-in prejudices. No matter what the law says, we are a youth-oriented society. True, selling is a profession in which performance counts more than anything else. However, the man or woman who *looks old,* at any age, is going to have to work harder for optimum performance. If you happen to look older, there may be something you can do to change the image. Maybe you wear glasses. Have you considered contacts? For many people, wearing contacts instead of glasses can subtract ten years from their apparent age.

Eye contact is important in selling, and contact lenses make such body language much more effective than do glasses. This is something you will especially want to check into if you wear thick glasses or if you wear bifocals because these tend to hide your eye expressions.

Some things seem a matter of such common sense that it seems everybody knows about them. Long-time sales managers have found that this "common" sense is, in fact, quite uncommon. Consider the matter of the car you drive, for example; or perhaps we should say the car you "wear" to work.

Wear Your Car Well

Perhaps it hasn't occurred to you that everything in your environment is part of what you "wear." Clients and prospects judge you according to the kind of car you drive. That doesn't mean that you have to drive a new car every year to gain the client's respect. However, you need to maintain your car in a manner that is consistent with good taste, not only to keep it in good mechanical condition. This means *keeping your car clean*. And it means *having needed body and paint work done as often as required.*

Your Metaclothing and You

Your client rarely buys anything from the "real" you. This is true because it is not the real you who is out there earning a living through selling—it is your *persona,* the personality you have created by living as a civilized human being. *You wear this persona on every sales call you make.* Perhaps it is unfair that YOU are judged by the "metaclothing" of this persona. But fair or not, it is a fact of life with which you must contend. How do you contend with this fact? By developing a keen awareness of it and then living in that awareness. It will be the mission of this book to help you to heighten that awareness as you read and study the lessons which follow.

LESSON NO. 6: THE TRUTH ABOUT POSITIVE THINKING

Of all the things that you must do prior to coming face to face with your customer, none is more important than the work you do on your own head: the mental preparation you should go through each day so that you will meet your clients, at the least, on equal footing. Perhaps these five minutes on positive thinking, together with the next lesson (on autosuggestion), are the two most important lessons in this chapter. Study them carefully, and review them often.

You Must Convince Your Subconscious Mind

Somebody once said that faith is believing what you know isn't so. If that is a correct definition of faith, then that's not what true positive thinking is. The kind of positive thinking that works is the kind which *operates from a subconscious level.* This is to say that you must first convince the subconscious layers of your mind before there can be a conscious acceptance.

The Influence of Time

It is believed that the subconscious doesn't know the meaning of time. In the subconscious realm, everything happens NOW. This means that you should imagine your goals being fulfilled NOW. At the same time, however, you will do most of your positive thinking about your *long-range goals*. Imagine where you want to be a year from now, but picture it happening now. The subconscious will seek to resolve this contradiction by moving you toward the life changes necessary to achieve that goal.

Concern Yourself
about ACTS, Not Results

Short-term goals should be the subject of your positive thinking, too. However, this time you should concern yourself more with what you DO than with what happens as a result of your action. Relinquish all responsibility for results, once you have made sure that *you are doing what you should be doing* to accomplish a certain result. Remember, unless the subconscious is convinced, your positive thinking will produce negative results. And the subconscious *will simply refuse highly improbable results*, like (say) a suggestion that you will be a millionaire by 9:00 A.M. tomorrow. It *will accept* the suggestion that *you will begin working in a new, more confident manner, starting now!*

Fake It till You Make It

You have to begin acting in your more confident manner before you actually feel this new confidence. Determine how you would act if you really believed that you were confident and assured in some certain situation. Then *begin at once to act in this manner*. Don't concern yourself that you don't quite pull it off at first. Don't worry about what others may think. You are building a pattern of confident action, laying down a network of electro-chemical action traces that the subconscious workings of your mind will use in similar situations when they come up. Soon the *feel of confidence* will follow.

Put It in Writing

The mind believes what it sees in writing. Begin at once to write the truth about yourself; both the truth that is now manifest for you and everybody else to see, and the truth that you feel will soon make itself known. Remember the caveat about long-range versus short-range goals. First write a vivid description of what you expect your life will be like when you will have attained your long-range goal. Describe the objects, circumstances, and conditions of your life as you imagine they will be. Spend some time on this, and do it over as many times as you have to, to get it right. Describe everything as though it were in existence *now*. *Put all the verbs in the present tense!*

Write an Action Plan

To have a plan of action means that you know what it takes to attain a specific goal. In designing your Action Plan, you will probably study the lives of others who have attained to the level of success to which you aspire. Write out a list of the personality and character qualities which you see in these role models. *Memorize this list of qualities.* Next, write a scenario, a detailed description of YOU performing in the desired manner. This is your short-range goal, one which you can reasonably expect to attain *now*.

For a more detailed treatment of the workings of the subconscious mind, I suggest you get a copy of the book *The Power of the Subconscious Mind,* by Joseph Murphy. You will also enjoy and profit from *The Secret of the Ages,* by Robert Collier. While I don't agree with everything that has been written about the subconscious mind, I have discovered much that works for me. You can't do it all in your head, but think right and then ACT—and you've got it made.

LESSON NO. 7: LEARN TO "DEHYPNOTIZE" YOURSELF

Don't Let Life's Chances Hypnotize You

If it were not for a lifetime of negative influences that need to be overcome, you would probably have no difficulty believing in yourself; that is, in thinking "positively" most of the time. But you have had those experiences. You know that there have been many times in your life when you really felt good about something; really were sure that you would achieve something, and yet you failed! If this happened only once or twice, the chances are that you shrugged it off, picked yourself up, and kept going. But what if it happened three or maybe five times in a row? The odds are that you would become "hypnotized" by this string of failures—mesmerized into believing something totally false about yourself.

This lesson will concern itself with giving you a few tips on how to neutralize the hypnotic influence of untoward life-chances. It will give you a technique which you can use not to "hypnotize" yourself into believing something that isn't so but to *dehypnotize* yourself so that what is really true about you will thoroughly saturate your consciousness. If the lesson succeeds in doing this, you will be able to recognize "failure" for what it is; simply a stumbling block on your upward path.

Unconscious Autosuggestion

As a sales professional, you don't expect that everybody will welcome you with open arms. Certainly you don't expect them to ask you to take out your orderbook the minute you walk in. If you've been at it awhile, you expect that many people (perhaps most people) will not buy your product or service. But you know by now that there are also a certain number of people who will buy; some of them even if you do everything wrong! However, since there is no way of knowing which customer will buy which time, you need to be especially careful that *you do not let what one prospect says affect what happens in the mind of some other prospect.* Go back and read that again. Memorize the words in italics.

I'm not talking about some sort of occult happening here. I'm not talking about ESP or anything like that. I'm talking about one prospect influencing another through the *medium of your mind!*

Silently Deny Every Negative Comment

You have no choice but to *hear* what a prospect tells you, be it good or bad—negative or positive. But you do have a choice about what you *listen to;* you do have a choice about *what you believe.* "Business is bad," your prospect tells you. You needn't contradict him or her for saying that. But don't reinforce the belief by agreeing. Don't even nod your head. Wait. When the negative tirade ends, say silently, *"I don't believe that."* Then proceed with your presentation. Every time your prospect jumps in with a negative comment, listen politely and say to yourself, "I don't believe that." Then continue as though nothing had happened.

Unconscious autosuggestion happens when you permit the negative beliefs of others to lodge *uncritically* in your consciousness. Just hearing a negative comment should have little effect on you. But *listening uncritically* can be disastrous! Don't argue with a prospect or client—not ever. Just silently repeat those magic words: *"I don't believe that."*

LESSON NO. 8: TOTAL RELAXATION THROUGH MEDITATION

Just a few years ago I would have hesitated to discuss this subject in a book like this. Meditation sounds . . . mystical. Or at least mysterious. It is, however, a perfectly natural physical and mental practice. I happen to believe that the mind controls the body, that what you think determines how you act and what you are. But even if your own belief is less "extreme" than this, you will probably agree that these two "systems"— body and mind—have a profound effect on each other. For example, you have undoubtedly noticed that when you are overly tired you don't think as clearly as when you are rested; fresh, as after a good night's sleep.

For many people it seems to be the other way around. People who do mostly mental work usually find that what happens in their heads determines whether they feel tired or rested. Meditation is a means of emptying the mind of its daily charge of tension. Although some of the things you do to enter the meditative state may seem strange, meditation offers a truly delightful way to relax both before a call, and at the end of a stressful day. I won't go into any great detail on the nuances of meditation here. If you would like to explore it more deeply, there are many good books on the subject in your bookstore or library. But let me at least tell you how to begin.

Meditate on a Meaningless Sound

This method requires that you focus your attention on some word or sound which will not call up an image that might set you off on a train of thought. Many people use a word like *one*. I like the sound *zot* for this purpose. You may want to invent your own sound.

To begin, seat yourself in a quiet place (if you can find one). Close your eyes and say quietly to yourself, "*zot*" (or whatever sound you have chosen). Then do it again. Ignore any thoughts that try to intrude. Keep saying your meaningless sound. Breathe deeply. You will probably be able to keep this up for no more than two or three minutes in the beginning, but keep trying. You will increase your ability to focus on *zot* as time goes by. When you get up to ten minutes or so without strain, you will come away from each session with a tremendous feeling of peace, rest, and relaxation. I can't explain why this is so; I can only urge that you try it for yourself.

Meditate on a "Blank Field"

This second method is more difficult for some people. In this method, the concentration is directed toward a visual "field" rather than toward a sound. The description of the practice may sound silly to you. It will look even sillier to anyone who sees you doing it. Never mind that—do it anyhow.

Here's what you do: Take a ping-pong ball and cut it exactly in half. Try to be as neat as you can in this operation; having two really accurately halved sections is very important. Once you have accomplished this, you are ready to use the two plastic hemispheres in your meditative practice. To do this, place yourself in a comfortable position as before. But this time, be sure you are facing a fairly strong light source. Now, lean your head back, and place one ping-pong ball over each eye.

Okay—I said was going to sound silly. Are you done laughing now? Good! Then let's get on with it. (By the way, I'm told that primitive people laugh when told about elevators.)

With the hemispheres of plastic in place over each eye, press them down so that no light comes in underneath (this was the reason for being so careful in the cutting process). Now open your eyes, and try to keep from blinking. You will see nothing but a *blank field—a solid "sheet" of white light*. Remember, try not to blink your eyes. This will take practice, but eventually you will be rewarded by a most unusual experience: the "blank field" of light *will seem to wash over you!* You will see and feel the light as though it were *inside your head!*

Breathe deeply as you meditate on the light. As you learn to keep your eyes open, you will more and more feel a sense of immersion in the field of white light, and with this feeling will come a beautiful sensation of deep relaxation. Again, I don't know why it works. And, again, I urge you to try it.

LESSON NO. 9: STATE-OF-THE-ART SELLING

Some salespeople seem perfectly happy to continue plodding along, doing things in the same old way. Compare what the average salesperson does in the field with the way similar jobs are done in a modern office or in an up-to-date retail store.

The Audio List

A salesman in Michigan finds prospecting easier with a microcassette tape recorder. When he arrives in a town he hasn't worked before or hasn't worked in a long time, he does what he calls a "drive-through." He drives down the street slowly, with the micro in one hand. As he drives, he calls out the names of likely looking shops and stores. When he gets back to his base, he has an *audio list* of perhaps a hundred names. First he transcribes all the names; then he looks up the phone numbers and starts calling for appointments. He finds this system much quicker than looking through city directories and reference books, and finds that this visual, on-the-spot search is the best way to determine whether a particular firm is really worth calling on. Since he is telephoning people who are physically close to one another to begin with, his appointments will be much closer to one another than they would have been had he used an alphabetical list like the Yellow Pages.

The Audio Orderbook

You may feel that you absolutely must get your customer's signature at the time of the sale, but a Los Angeles tool salesman who "writes" orders by speaking them into his microcassette says this about it: "Customers accept delivery because they *want* the merchandise, not because of a signature on an order blank!"

By the way, this particular salesman does transcribe his orders, together with any required purchase order number, onto a regular sales form later on.

I've heard about a door-to-door cosmetic saleswoman who has carried the technology quite a bit further. I understand that she has one of the new personal computers at home, with a printer hooked up to it. She keyboards (types) her orders off of the cassette recording. The computer has been programmed not only to type out individdual delivery tickets, but to tally up the total sales, and to print out a list for her to order from the distributor at the end of the week.

Checking up on Yourself

Whether or not you are actually self-employed, the very nature of selling makes you your own boss most of the time. The truth is, however, that you are also *your own employee*. The microcassette gives you the opportunity to really study yourself. When you are using the micro for the purpose of recording customer orders, customers quickly come to accept the little machine and rarely feel self-conscious in its presence.

Take advantage of the opportunity to leave the machine on during your presentation every now and then. As you listen to yourself later, you will be able to spot those areas in which you need improvement.

The Ultimate Orderbook

I don't know of anybody using this device—*yet*. I'm talking about the little computers that you can carry with you and which enable you to communicate with your firm's computer via telephone. They are small enough to fit in a standard attaché case, and they provide such things as instant order transmission, inventory checking, keeping track of appointments and schedules, and many other features.

You may feel that your product or service doesn't warrant all of this "fancy stuff." Perhaps not. Maybe your competitor's product does.

LESSON NO. 10:
THE NAMES OF THE GAME

Learn Those Buzz Words

Maybe you can't learn as much about your customer's business as he or she knows. But you can try! At the very least, you can learn to speak the language your client speaks. You can learn the names of products, processes, and services. You probably have already formed the habit of vocabulary building by writing down and looking up "plain English" words with which you are not familiar. Begin now to do the same with those special words your client uses in talking about his or her business.

Associate Names with Departmental Titles

There is no substitute for rehearsal and drill when it comes to memorizing, but learning to associate names with titles can be a temporary shortcut. Suppose that a Fred Boaz is head of the machine shop. Picture a huge buzzing machine (*Boaz-buzz*). Or if a Ms. Fillmore is head of the accounting department, you could picture that her pockets are bulging—"filled more" now that she's in charge of accounting.

An aid for memorizing is the *endless-loop tape*. These tapes are made for use in telephone-answering machines, but they will work on standard cassette recorders. On each tape there is just enough space to record, say, ten or twenty names. When you play them back, the tape keeps playing the names, instead of stopping at the end of the tape.

As you record the names, pause slightly between the name and the title. Here's the reason for this suggestion. You will play a little game with yourself: As you hear a name (on playback), try to respond with the correct title before the recording gives the title. You may want to make a second tape—the reverse of the first tape, in that it would give the *titles* first. You will be pleasantly surprised at how quickly and easily you can learn long lists of names, lists of technical terms, names of departments, and other, normally unassociated data using the tape recorder and an endless-loop tape.

"What Are Your Initials?"
and Other Tricks That Don't Work

Some salespeople attempt to disguise the fact that they don't care enough about the prospect's business to memorize important data like terms, titles, and names. I know you've had it happen to you that someone you buy from regularly—say your druggist or your cleaner—will ask, with hand poised above the salesbook, "What are your initials?"

Well, you just ask a department head what his or her initials are, and you're likely to get a response like "J.G." (or whatever); you're still stuck! Another point: Maybe the plant engineer is accustomed to having his workers call him "Chief," but you'd better learn his name, if you ever want to sell him.

The whole subject of *nicknames* in the industrial setting is an interesting one. I once spent several years working in the printing plant of a large publishing company. Many of the typesetters and press operators called one another by names like "Red," "Blackie," "Bozo," "Plum," "Cherry." I even knew one man who was sometimes referred to as "Cab," which was short for "Cabbage Head"! You may think that these are terms of friendly endearment. Sometimes they are. But if you want to check this out, ask a simple question: "What does your family call you?" "Cab" was always called "Bill" by his wife. "Red" was known as "Jim" by his wife.

LESSON NO. 11: THE GENTLE ART
OF NAME DROPPING

Forgetting Names Is a Luxury

Forgetting names is the kind of luxury that results in an extravagant waste of good prospects and valuable clients. If you have made up your mind to earn your living at selling, know this: Failing to remember names is the kind of profligacy that can quickly strip a valuable sales territory of its profit-producing potential. Get this clear: *You absolutely must remember names and faces.* There are several good books on the market which can help you to use your memory more effectively. Most of these systems depend on associating names with faces. The more outlandish the image, the easier it will be for you later to recall the name. These systems do work, but some find that the results are not long-lasting.

I was once involved in promoting such a memory system. The man who had developed this particular system had also written a book on it and was going from town giving seminars on how to remember names and faces. To prove the efficacy of his method he had recruited me and several other locals and taught us the system. We then demonstrated to groups like employees of banks and department stores how "anybody" could learn to remember names and faces.

I must say, I was much impressed by my new-found ability. But a couple of days later a group from the largest bank in town happened to be eating lunch in the same restaurant where my mentor and I were having lunch. I recognized the faces of several in the group, but couldn't recall one name! And neither could the memory expert. Fortunately, someone from the sponsoring organization walked up at that time and broke into the conversation before the painful truth became too obvious.

Perhaps you have heard the story about the memory expert who had met a Mrs. Kelly. "This one will be easy to remember," he said to himself as he associated Mrs. Kelly's name with her rather large belly. Later on he ran into her again and nodded his head politely. "Ah," he said, "so nice to see you again, Mrs. Bass."

In spite of the obvious drawbacks, memory systems based on these kinds of associations can be useful. The *solution* to the problem, however, lies in a better understanding of the way our memories work to begin with.

Short-Term Versus Long-Term Memory

Most memory systems fail to take into account certain basics of learning theory. Associating a name with a face or with the name of a company will help to store the name in short-term memory. And there is one major problem connected with that. Everything that is packed into short-term memory shoves out something that is already there! In fact, without extreme diligence even long-term memory may be affected. (As in the case of the college professor or ichthyology. He complained that every time he learned the name of a new student, he forgot the name of a fish.)

Learning theorists estimate that short-term memory will hold approximately seven separate items, which will be lost *unless committed to long-term memory by rehearsal.* To really nail down those names requires work. This means that you will have to rehearse new names at the first opportunity. And the longer you want to remember the names, the more you will have to rehearse them. Until you are sure that you have committed those names to memory, carry a name book.

Dropping Names Is Easy When You Remember

You need to be able to "drop" names easily, glibly. When you are in a position to say, "Frank Smith at Citywide had a similar problem, and he solved it this way," you are not just making a claim, you are telling a real-life story that will be believed. The same story without a name would fall flat.

LESSON NO. 12: STUDY, SCRIPT WRITING, AND ROLE PLAYING

Quit Reading and Start Studying

Probably you have read several, perhaps *many* books on salesmanship. Why are you reading yet another? Are you really reading in hopes of finding something new? Perhaps there is something new here, but if you only *read* this book *you will not find it!* There is a great difference between *understanding* new material and really *learning* it. Please believe me: *learning means memorizing.*

The Road to the Subconscious Mind

Only when you have learned a subject so well that the material of the subject becomes part of your very nature can it truly be said that you have learned it. In other words, effective *professional* selling comes from deep—subconscious—levels. Memorization is the path that leads to the subconscious. Memorize your basic sales talk. Know it so well that you could give it in your sleep. Does this mean giving a "canned" presentation? Not if you do it right. If you fear that knowing what you are going to say will destroy your spontaneity, your freshness, think for a moment on the manner in which a good actor or actress delivers lines. Does your favorite television or screen star's performance sound canned?

You will want to write out and learn your sales talk in such a manner that you will learn it in "packets," rather than learning a complete presentation from start to finish. There are several reasons for doing this.

Your prime reason for learning small segments of the talk by heart instead of learning the whole talk as a unit is that this is the way in which you will deliver it. After you deliver each segment, you will pause and elicit feedback from your prospect. When you have answered your prospect's questions, you will slip easily into the next segment.

Write a Script for the Main Characters

The main characters are, of course, you and your prospect. Be sure to write your script in dialog form. Deliver about a hundred words, come to some kind of climax, then ask questions which will get your prospect to respond. You needn't pay a great deal of attention to what the prospect says during the early responses. For the most part, those comments you hear in the beginning are just stock comments. You see, your *prospect* is really using a "canned" presentation—one that is designed to put salespeople off. This is not to suggest that prospects never tell the truth when they make objections. However, a good sign that early objections are spurious is this: The second time you get an objection, it is usually not the same objection! Here is an important point to remember: *Don't answer any of these early objections.* Simply paraphrase what the prospect said to show that you were listening. Then go on with your talk.

Use Your Tape Recorder
for Creative Role Playing

Learning should be fun! You should write your presentation as though you were writing a play that you expected to see acted out on television. Write your part and the prospect's part so that you will have a script for each of you. The prospect's part will have cues so that your spouse or a friend can play the part of the prospect, throwing you an objection at certain spots in your presentation simply by reading the objection from the script.

Your tape recorder can be pressed into service to play the part of the prospect. You will want to make several "objection" tapes so that you will never know what objection is coming up next. Buy the C-10 computer tapes (which play for only five minutes on each side). You can get several objections on each side of the tape, and the tape takes just a couple of seconds to rewind. Use the "pause" switch to turn the machine on and off before and after each "objection." It can be a lot of fun practicing your role by using your script and a tape player in this manner. When learning is fun it is not only more thorough, but it happens much faster.

LESSON NO. 13: YOUR VOICE—WHAT KIND OF SELLING JOB DOES IT DO?

How Do You Sound over the Phone?

Most people who hear themselves on tape for the first time ask, "Is that the way I sound?" Well, the way your voice sounds in a recording cannot be exactly the way you hear it while you are speaking. As you speak, your voice sets up certain resonances in the bones of your head. You also hear these resonances, but the microphone doesn't pick them all up. What you hear when you play the recording back is more like what *others* hear when you speak to them. This fact can be of immense benefit to you if you wish to improve your telephone technique.

If you spend much time on the telephone, you will want to know how people hear you. There are a number of devices you can use to hear your voice *as it sounds to persons on the other end of the line*. One such device is a simple suction cup mike which plugs into your tape recorder. Another device automatically turns your recorder on every time you pick up the phone. If you have a telephone-answering machine, it may also provide a mechanism for recording two-way conversations—most of them do.

How to Avoid Charges of "Electronic Eavesdropping"

You don't need any special understanding of electronics to hook up any of these devices. You are required, however, to inform the telephone company that you have done so. And there is one more caution: You wouldn't want to run afoul of any federal or local laws. You should not secretly record any telephone conversation—*even one in which you participate!*

I inform people when I am recording the conversation in such a manner that the person's acquiescence becomes part of the recorded conversation. This means that my recorder has to be on and running the moment I begin the conversation. I say something like this: "I've turned my recorder on so that I don't miss any of this. You don't mind, do you?" Nobody has ever objected. Of course, if the call is simply a social call, I just switch the machine off. You could also go through all the pleasantries first, and when you are ready to begin recording, switch the machine on and say, "Just a second. Do you mind if I record this so I won't forget it?" Either way, you have the whole conversation on tape, for reference and study. And you have a record of the person's permission. No one has ever objected to my making these recordings.

There's Nothing Like the Real Thing

Admittedly, nothing beats doing your stuff in front of a prospect. A potential airline pilot could spend half a lifetime training in simulators, and he might never develop the courage to assume the responsibility for a cockpit command. This is why the would-be pilot must spend time as a copilot before being given a command.

If you are not afraid to call on customers, if you are totally fearless when it comes to making cold calls, you are indeed blessed. On the other hand, if you are like most of us who would like to *skip* that first three or four minutes in front of a prospect, have heart—there is help. Persistent practice will work. It did for me and for countless salespeople I have spoken with. And using tape recorders as I have suggested will be of immeasurable help to you in this battle.

Remember, fear feeds on fear; confidence on faith. Faithfully perform these suggested practices, and *you will see a marvelous change come over you*. Believe me, I know about this.

Give It Time to Work

Carry a microcassette into the field and use it. Record a complete presentation at least once a day. Compare some of these real sessions with the tapes you made of your dry runs earlier. Never be satisfied with your progress. Remember that there is a tremendous difference being *pleased* and being *satisfied*.

LESSON NO. 14:
A SUSPECT IS NOT A PROSPECT

Quit Calling on Suspects

It is simply not true that *everybody* is a prospect for your product or services, no matter what you sell. It may be true that everybody is a *suspect*, but that is vastly different. I know an office-supply store owner who decided to hire an outside salesperson. Finally, someone was hired on a straight commission basis and was told that he should call on every business firm in town. It is theoretically true that almost every business place uses office supplies. But this salesman soon discovered that there are hundreds of retailers who not only didn't own a typewriter—they didn't need one! Many of these small store owners ordered from wholesalers by telephone. Also, the only charge accounts they had were those of national credit-card users. They rarely wrote letters, so they had minimal need for such things as typewriters, stationery, carbon paper, typewriter ribbons, and file folders. It was then that this sales rep realized that his customer profile should not say simply "business owner," but "business owner who writes letters."

Write a Customer Profile

Before you set foot in your territory, you should know what you hope to find there. Is your typical customer old, middle-aged, or young? Male or female? Married or single? You may think that your customer profile can be drawn broadly enough to fit any or all of these categories. But you should know to which group *most of your good customers belong.* Draw your customer profile so that it describes your really good customers, and resolve that henceforth you will seek to make sure that almost all of your prospecting is directed toward finding more such customers.

Good Prospects Come from Good Customers

One of the best places to start prospecting is in the store, shop, office, or home of one of your best customers. The chances are that the customer belongs to some organization and has met other people who are similarly situated. A powerful, partially nonverbal technique for securing good leads from good customers is to ask right after you have packed to leave. Walk to the door, then stop and come back in. Pull out a pad and pen, and say something like, "Would you mind giving me the name of another successful person like yourself who might also be able to use this?" Then give the customer some categories to think in: "Like your attorney? Or your CPA? Or somebody you know in your club?" Once you have asked, keep quiet, keep your pen poised, wait. The nonverbal, subtle message here is that you're not leaving until you get a couple of names.

Ask Your Friends

Personal friends can be a good source of profitable leads. Just be sure to really define the kind of prospect you are looking for. Otherwise, you may wind up with a list of *suspects* instead of prospects. Remember, just *one* good prospect name is worth a whole list of suspects. You can get *suspects* just by leafing through the pages of any phone book. So that you will be absolutely clear about what kind of prospect name you are going to solicit from your friend, *memorize your customer profile.*

There is a special way of asking for these names. Always describe your prospect first, before asking for names. If you ask first, your friend may start giving you names right away. Then you will find yourself in the uncomfortable position of having to reject your friend's suggestions. Some people freeze up when this happens; they couldn't give you more names even if they wanted to. To prevent this from happening, try describing your prospect:

"You probably know somebody who has been in business for five years or so and is in the million-dollar-a-year category, don't you?"

If you will practice this technique until you can quickly define your prospect in terms of your customer profile, you will be able to ask for leads in the natural, self-confident manner that produces results.

LESSON NO. 15:
DO YOU REALLY LIKE SELLING?

Love What You're Doing,
Learn to Love It—or Quit!

No matter how much time you spend on "technique," it all boils down to one thing: Do you really *want* to do this thing that you are preparing yourself to do? If you don't, you can study and you can practice for the rest of your life, but you will never really succeed. Selling is one of the most difficult professions to succeed at in the first place. Yet it is one of the easiest to get into. One reason for this is the "results count" attitude of employers of salespeople. This is especially true where salespeople are hired on the straight commission basis. Simply put, if a firm has to pay a salesperson only when something is sold, the screening and selection process takes place, more often than not, *after* the salesperson is hired. As one sales manager put it, "If you sell, you eat." Presumably, this system eliminates misfits in a hurry. But does it? It is true that those who are so grossly unsuited to the field that they can't make enough sales to keep body and soul together are soon eliminated. Yet there remains a residuum who exist on the borderline—some for years—earning just enough to get by and probably hating every minute of it.

Money Is Not Enough

If you are in sales—or anything else—just to earn a living, you are working below your full potential. Now, you may *love* the challenge of making money, and that could provide you with the motivation you need. And you may *love* money itself and the things that it will buy. That, too, could do the trick. But selling has its dry spells. What will keep you going when you haven't made a sale for days? If you have become a salesperson because of a strong feeling for the sales process itself—if you truly love what you are doing rather than being overly concerned with the money involved—you will have what it takes to persist when the going gets tough.

Inherent Rewards Motivate Top Achievers

When you approach a new prospect for the first time, is it with a sense of dread or with a sense of adventure? Are you just as happy over what your client gets from a sale as you are over what you get? You should be. But there's another test that may not be so easy for you to pass. How do you feel when a really big sale has slipped through your fingers, but you know it was because your product or service just wasn't right for this client? Are you actually *glad* when clients don't buy something which isn't right for them? (Even from you?)

Should You Be Doing Something Else?

Even when you love what you are doing, there will be some things that you will love less than others. This is no problem if the job itself is not contrary to your own inner nature. If you are a basically enthusiastic person, you should have little difficulty raising yourself at least to a state of *willingness* over those unpleasant tasks involved in a job which you really like. "Know thyself" is the best advice anybody can give you here. When you make a sale, do you feel like hurrying to your next call before the client changes his or her mind? Do you ever experience a sense of guilt over a large sale? Ask yourself this question: "Is there something else that I would rather be doing for a living?" If you have answered in the affirmative, take a hard look at what you are doing. Maybe you shouldn't be selling.

Would You Do It for Free?

Here is a "success formula" that seems to summarize this lesson well: *Find the work you like so well that you would do it without pay if you could. Then become so good at it that somebody will gladly pay you well for doing it.*

You will recall the admonition that *you should love selling, learn to love it, or get out of it.* You can only begin from where you are right now in the selling profession. If you don't quite have the *conviction* that this is where you belong, be of good cheer: There may yet be hope! Ask yourself this question: "Is there *anything* about selling that I really like? Anything I like *very much?*" Build on what you find. Maybe you can move, one step at a time; *tolerate* some things and ignore others. *If you have gumption and determination, you may yet learn to love it!*

LESSON NO. 16:
THE THREE KINDS OF SALESPEOPLE

It is, I believe, very difficult to become a top professional salesperson unless you love selling (even if you have had to learn to love it). There are, however, ranks in this profession as there are in any other. There are *grades* of proficiency to which you may aspire in turn.

The Order Taker

Sales managers often use the expression *order taker* as a pejorative. But *somebody* has to do the work of taking orders for such things as industrial uniforms and shop towels; *somebody* has to drive bread trucks, cold-drink trucks, milk trucks.

However, there is a class of order takers that I call the "order takers looking for a job." These are people who pretend to serious salesmanship by holding down a job alongside serious professionals while they spend half of their time looking for other employment. These are the kinds of sales reps who will write orders if customers insist on it; the kinds of salespersons who *devour* leads, trying to find customers who are ready to buy, rather than spending the time needed to convert initial interest to strong desire for the product or service.

The Technician

Perhaps most of the long-time members of many sales organizations belong to this group. These are people who understand the intricacies of a firm's products and who know how to make effective selling presentations. Understand, I am not talking about people who understand how to *repair* the product—or how to install it. I'm referring to those who have, by dint of incessant practice, mastered the routine involved in making good demonstrations. I'm talking about people who have calculated *how many* such demonstrations it takes to make a sale and who then proceed *to make this number of demonstrations,* come hell or high water!

There is another thing that technicians are noted for. They have an almost unshakeable faith in the law of averages—in the working out of the rules of probability. They are often careful record keepers and so aren't thrown off by lucky streaks; neither by streaks of bad luck nor of good luck. Technicians experiencing a string of easy sales know how to take it for what it is. They aren't lulled into slacking off when this happens, for they know how a string of easy ones may easily be followed by an equally long string of tough ones. *No matter what, technicians keep on keeping on.* An order taker may say, "Hey! I've made more in two days than I usually make in a week. I'll just take off the rest of the week." The technician? Never!

The Professional

It is my conviction that no more than 20 percent of a sales organization are in this group. Perhaps you have heard this before: *20 percent of the sales usually come from 80 percent of the sales force; 80 percent of the sales come from 20 percent of the sales force.* This is called the *80–20 (or 20–80) rule.* I have met many sales managers over the years—*almost all of them agree that this formulation is correct!*

Professionals, of course, do all of the things that technicians do. However, what they do, they do much more efficiently. And they do things that technicians never even *think* of doing. But if there is one general statement that you could make about professional sales reps, it is this: Almost without exception, *they think of themselves as pros.* They think, look, and act like the pros of other fields. The professional sales rep has the bearing of the person who knows where he or she is going and knows how to get there. But what makes the pro so *special*? What makes the kind of person who consistently outproduces the merely *good* salesperson by a factor of *three,* or *four,* or *five*? This is the subject of the next lesson.

LESSON NO. 17:
THE FIVE MARKS OF A SALES PRO

As a salesman, sales manager, and sales writer, I have worked with, trained, and interviewed more salespeople than I can count. Always I have asked myself the question, "What makes this tremendous difference in ability and in income—this difference between the *good* salesperson and the *expert;* the *professional*?" I have been asking this question for years, and I am not certain that I am even *close* to a final answer. However, I have found *five important characteristics* that all pros I have known seem to share. For what this is worth, I list them below. You may want to remember these five characteristics and seek to make them part of your consciousness from here on out.

1. *Energy.* True professionals do *everything with a special "bounce" and alacrity.* And they seem to have the strength and endurance to keep on doing it for hours after "good" salespeople have called it a day. You may know a top pro who works no more than forty hours a week. Almost all I have known regularly work *at least sixty hours;* seventy or eighty hours is not at all unusual.

2. *Fervor.* Pros have *fervor.* This is more than enthusiasm. They have the enthusiastic attitude, of course. But they have also developed a *hot belief* in what they are doing. This belief is often so strong that true pros sometimes have difficulty "turning it off."

3. *Polish.* This is a difficult quality to describe in words, but it is perhaps the one quality you will never fail to recognize. Is it a matter of attire? It's more than that—although the person who has polish will certainly be a fastidious dresser. What about manners—speech? One could certainly not exhibit polish *without* impeccable manners, careful use of the language. Yet it is more. It is being well dressed *without ostentation.* It is speaking carefully *without affectation.* It is being polite *without condescension.* And it is more.

4. *Credibility.* Professional sales reps are *believable.* There is almost no way that you can prove every statement of benefit you will make about your product or service. If you are a good mechanic or technician, you will know a lot about those benefits you can prove, and you will know instantly how to bring these proofs into play when needed. You will know what to do and when to do it—that's all part of technical ability; all part of the *mechanics* of the job of selling.

The pro, however, brings another dimension to this business, to the *profession* of selling. It is not something he or she does; it is more *a matter of being.*

You are believable when you totally believe in what you are saying, in what you are selling. Some sales pros have this quality in such measure that they need demonstrate (or "prove") only about one assertion in ten. How high is your "BQ," your Believability Quotient?

5. *Momentum.* Here's a special point you may want to remember. Top pros who stay with one line long enough almost always reach a point where the "system" takes over. That is, they come to a spot on their path where the things they have done before begin, seemingly, to work on their own. Calls they have made over and over; demonstrations they have made; friendships formed; loyalties built; goodwill engendered—all come together and *work for the pro who has done the extra work required* to build momentum.

Momentum is the impetus that a moving object has that keeps it moving unless something slows it down or stops it. If you throw a ball you don't have to run alongside it and pull (or push) it to keep it going. It's the same with the kind of momentum you will eventually build up as you work your territory. You are taking the professional approach when you work hard enough and long enough *each day* to build momentum into your territory.

LESSON NO. 18:
HOW TO SELL THE APPOINTMENT

Watch Those "Easy Ones"

It's easy to get the easy ones, hard to get the hard ones when you make telephone appointments. Many beginning salespeople have had to learn this one the hard way: If you push *just a little,* many "suspects" will say something like, "Okay. Come on by, and we'll take a look at what you have." After four or five hours on the phone this kind of "appointment" begins to sound a lot better than a flat "NO," or a curt "Not interested." It may *sound* better, but it could actually be much worse! Mark this well: People who are too easy on the phone are that way because, frequently, *they have no intention of giving your proposition serious consideration.*

There is, fortunately, a way of avoiding the so-called easy ones. This can be summed up in one word: *qualify.* There are many ways of doing this. Here's a method I've used myself:

"Mr. Jones, I suppose you could characterize what I sell as a 'sales training program' for your outside salespeople. But that's only because people like to give names to everything. What it really is, is a *device* that your salespeople use to train themselves—and to do this in *about one-fourth the time* that they would do it by the old trial-and-error method. I won't ask you to make a decision on this over the phone—it's too good for that. Could you give me about ten minutes tomorrow morning?"

The "Fuller Brush" Appointment Approach

This method is an old one, but it still works as an effective appointment-getting tool. It was a favorite of Fuller Brush sales reps.

A Fuller Brush Man (that's what they were called during my term as field sales manager for this fine old firm) setting up appointments for the next day's work would bounce up the steps with a good deal of commotion, then knock loudly on the door. When the housewife answered, he would say pleasantly, but with force:

"Fuller Brush! Here's your new catalog!" Then he would *take a step backwards* and hold the catalog out, waiting for the housewife to open the door and take the catalog. He wouldn't say another word until the housewife had either taken the catalog or had offered some kind of reason for not accepting it. Usually she accepted it. Then he would take another step backwards (to remain totally nonthreatening). Next he said:

"Please look over the catalog when you get a chance. I'll stop back tomorrow to see if you need anything from it. Also, I have an exciting new sample to give you when I come back. I'll see you at 9:27 in the morning. Okay?" There seemed to be something about that "odd-minute gambit" that put a value on his time, made the housewife think twice about agreeing to the appointment if she knew she was not going to be home.

The same technique works with business calls. The application is slightly different, but the principle is the same.

Using the Catalog Technique on Business Calls

You could never make the number of demonstrations in a day that old-time brush salespeople made (forty or fifty!), and some of the urgency from the odd-minute appointment approach is missing here. But these are only slight differences. Here's how one salesman uses the technique. He sells advertising specialties such as ballpoint pens, book matches, keychains, and assorted imprinted specialties.

"The shops I call on are usually small enough so that there are maybe one or two clerks—usually younger people. I just walk up to the most mature-looking person I see and say, 'This is your shop, isn't it?' More than half the time I'm right. If I am, I hold out a brochure and say, 'You may find something in here that will help you to sell more merchandise. Look it over, and I'll check with you later to see if there is anything you'd like to ask me about.' Since I'm not putting any strings on it, most people accept the book without protest. As I walk away, I say, 'There are some really unusual business builders in that little booklet. I'll be finished next door at 2:25. I'm marking this stop down for 2:27. I'll stop by and leave you a free sample. Okay?' "

LESSON NO. 19:
THE GOLDEN GIFT OF HABIT

Habit Frees the Conscious Mind

Your selling efficiency will skyrocket when certain practices become habitual. What are these practices? Many of them are recommended in this book. The secret of making these practices habitual may be one that you have already discovered.

The most important secret in the formation of beneficial new habits is called the *no exception rule.* It states: During the early stages of habit formation, *always perform the desired act in the way in which you expect to perform it later under the control of habit.* Remember, the important key word here is *always!* Once the habit becomes firmly established, you may vary its performance if reason suggests that you should. No great harm will then be done by occasionally deviating from your procedure. However, while you are still in the habit-formation stage, *just one* deviation can wreck your program! Ignorance of this important fact has been the death of many well-intended programs.

Some behaviorists theorize that repeated actions "etch" neural traces that are not very deep in the beginning, but deepen with time *if the actions persist and no exceptions intervene that permit the system to recover.* Once the "grooves" are deep enough, the circuitry will be there for the action to take place without the need for conscious choice; the synapses will fire in your nervous system each time the proper stimulus is present, and you will do what you are supposed to do while your conscious mind attends to something else.

Of course, much of behavioral science is still theory. Maybe when you hear or read the word "theory" you substitute the word "guesswork." Scientists prefer to think of theories as conceptual models. A model is a replica of some real structure, and no model is true in every detail to the structure it represents. A scale model auto, for example, may seem to be like the real object—until one examines it closely. But for all of its drawbacks and failures, the model helps us to understand the real structure better.

The conceptual model helps us to understand other connected facts. At least it helps us to think about these facts in a useful and meaningful way. And that's good enough for me. I wouldn't even need to know *why* habits work as they do. My own experience has taught me the truth before I "understood" it: Many habits had served to simplify my life. I only learned those habits consciously when I practiced them without permitting exceptions. Just *performing* these suggested practices *without exception* will do the same for you.

You Don't Forget to Do Things
That Have Become Habitual

I have said earlier that you should get the list-making habit. I believe that you should. But don't clutter your lists with things that you should be doing from habit. You undoubtedly know many people who never read a book without marking it. Some people use yellow highlighters for this purpose, marking so many passages that there is more yellow in the book than there is white! Others take copious notes as they read. I am going to ask that you don't write in this book, don't highlight it. These practices are okay, but they simply don't go far enough. They are no substitute for the kind of study that assists in the formation of profitable work habits. Instead, do the one thing that is practically guaranteed to help you form these habits: *memorize important passages, and practice them at the first opportunity.* Use your tape recorder as an aid to this memorizing. Memorize all of the italicized phrases and headlines. Don't just read, *study* and *form habits*.

2

How to PIQUE
the Passive Prospect

Almost nobody is glad to see a stranger walk in with a briefcase. However, the social niceties required for doing business may cause you to believe otherwise at times. Be assured: Your prospects will be passive at best, and you'll have to do something special to move them off of dead center before you have a chance to interest them in your proposition. They are thinking their own thoughts when you walk up; they want to go on thinking them and would just as soon not think the thoughts you wish to offer them.

These lessons will show you how to break down that barrier of preoccupation behind which your prospects are hiding, how to get them to *attend to* the matter in which you hope to interest them, and how to lead them—step by step—to the point at which you will begin to create this interest.

LESSON NO. 20:
THE "SERVICE" OPENER

Make Free Repairs

While it is true that the "stranger with a briefcase" is rarely welcome, you probably know that there are things you can do that will quickly remove you from the "stranger" category. Probably the most effective attention-getter in the pro's bag of tricks is the *free service* opener. To use this opener you will have to learn enough about your product (as well as the competitive substitutes for it) to qualify as an expert. And you will have to keep abreast of the newest technology, to be sure that your free service doesn't do any harm.

Such service needn't be elaborate to be effective and appreciated. A typewriter and office-supply salesman gets a lot of attention with a "$1.00 COA [Clean, Oil, and Adjust] Special." Strictly speaking, this is not quite a free service. But he claims that he got fewer takers "for free" than he gets when he charges this nominal amount. In addition to this, the $1.00 charge gives him an excuse to pull out his orderbook! While his orderbook is out and he's writing in it, he also suggests things like ribbons, paper, and hand cleaner. A one-dollar "sale" can easily turn into a fifty- or one-hundred-dollar order in a hurry.

Give Free (But Usable) Advice

You've heard it said that free advice is worth every bit of what it costs. That's probably true when it comes to *personal* advice. Business advice, or technical advice, is something else. If you are a dedicated professional, you have a wealth of information that your clients should be happy to possess. If you are in a position to pass some of this advice on without charge, the chances are good that your prospective client will be most appreciative and will likely express this appreciation by doing something for you in return (like giving you an order).

Attract Attention by Spreading the News

A woman selling computer software products makes sure she is always welcome by seeing that her prospects are kept up-to-date on the latest developments in the computer industry. She is a voracious reader and goes through several computer magazines a month, digesting information and taking notes. She has her own personal computer, and using this she prints a two-page newsletter every two or three weeks. Although she is too busy to worry about things like regular publication dates, her customers still look forward to this free publication (which she hand-delivers, of course).

How to Package Free Information

Half of the battle of getting your clients and prospects to appreciate the value of your free information is won when you learn the art of packaging. The computer saleswoman learned that her newsletter was better received when she punched it to fit a three-ring binder, then presented the binder along with a half-dozen back numbers to her clients.

Satisfy Curiosity and You Lose Attention

Simply arousing curiosity is really not all that difficult. *Sustaining* it requires considerably more effort. Curiosity must be sustained for it to be of value in the sales process, for it is a truism that *when you satisfy curiosity you lose attention.* You can sustain attention through the *delayed-explanation technique.*

A printing salesman has a type slug which he uses to arouse curiosity when he opens his presentation. A type slug usually has a letter, number, or other symbol on it in reverse and is used in the letterpress process of printing. However, this particular type slug had *the entire Lord's Prayer* etched on its printing face! With the naked eye one could discern only a roughened surface. But the salesman carried a powerful glass (a magnifier) with him; under the glass one could easily read the mirror image of this famous prayer.

In order to sustain curiosity he tied his explanation of the technology of camera reductions, engraving, and so on to the making of this special piece of type. But he *never satisfied curiosity* by actually showing the Lord's Prayer under the magnifier until his prospect had heard his entire presentation.

What to Do with It Once You've Got It

You'll need to practice this to get it right. (Use your tape recorder.) You can't just refuse to explain a thing that has piqued your prospect's curiosity and grabbed his attention, can you? *Yes, you can!* But you would never let him know that you so refused. The printing salesman uses a method which not only sustains the prospect's curiosity and attention but *intensifies* it. He picks the slug up, along with the magnifier, several times during the presentation—as though he is going to show it.

"Let Me Explain How This Trick Works"

Browsing through a magic shop can be an eye-opener. You're sure to find some curiosity-arousing items. I saw a woman selling "unbreakable" combs at a county fair. She had a little plastic mouse which crawled up her arm, climbed out of a drinking glass, walked from one hand to another, etc. As she said, you never had to wind it up or put gas in it. Her prospective customers (adults and children alike) were spellbound. Then she said, "Here, let me show you how this trick works. But first, let me show you something else that's rather magical." Then she demonstrated her unbreakable combs. When she had finished her demonstration, she said, "And everybody who buys a set of combs gets the Wonder Mouse as a free gift. But first, let me show you how it works." Her table was nearly turned over by people moving in to get a better look. Would YOU like to know how the mouse worked? Well, there was this little, almost invisible "something" which was about the size of a pea. She called it the "motor" . . . . But why don't you go down to your nearest magic store and ask about it?

LESSON NO. 22:
HIT THE GROUND RUNNING

Just Start Talking

This opener works because it catches the prospect off guard. If you walk in cold, almost anyone who greets you expects that you are either a customer or, if not, you will introduce yourself and state the name of the company you are working for. And it's okay if you do that. However, if you want to really *grab attention,* try the "start talking" routine. That means just walk up to your prospect and begin talking about some especially striking benefit which your product or service offers.

Overwhelm Them with Confidence

The salesperson who masters this opener quickly surrounds himself or herself with an aura of confidence. I saw this opener used for the first time while I was managing a floor-covering sales operation in Houston. I was looking over carpet samples that a wholesaler's salesman was showing me when a young man walked in. He didn't stop to talk to anybody else; he simply surmised that I was "in charge" and walked up to me. He handed me a fistful of ballpoint pens and said, "We have ten thousand misprinted pens like these. They're good; they write. They're just printed wrong. You can have them all for a nickel apiece."

I didn't buy the pens. I'm not even sure he had that many to sell. But then he shrugged off my "No," and he effortlessly—smoothly—

moved right into a presentation of his other advertising specialty products. And I did place an order.

Don't Ask for the Manager

Don't ever ask for "the manager" or "the buyer." This is a killer question. When you walk up, *you're* in charge. The moment you admit you *don't know* something as important as the identity of owner or manager of the establishment, you lose control. Now somebody else has to take over and furnish you with the information you need to regain control. You can count on this: Nobody wants to put you back in control!

The situation here is different than it would be if you were simply prospecting, hunting for leads and learning names for a future call. A goodly portion of humility would even be in order then. In this case, however, it's the confident air that wins the day. You establish and maintain that air when you create and sustain the impression that you know what's what and who's who.

Who Appears to Be "in Charge"?

It's often easy to spot the person in charge. Just try doing this, and you'll see what I mean. Even if you're wrong, what can you lose? Even flunkies aren't insulted if they're suddenly treated with a little respect—treated like they own the place. And if you make a mistake, somebody will set you straight. Likely there will be some comment like, "Oh, you'll have to talk to Mr. Jones about that." So what? Now you've got a name to work with.

LESSON NO. 23:
COLOR, MOTION, AND NOISE

When There's No Time for Subtlety

There are three basic and classic attention-getters. While you may feel that these attention-grabbers are too bold for your personality, you should at least know and understand them. These three attention-getters are; *(1) vivid color; (2) rapid motion;* and *(3) loud noise.*

The Attention-Grabbing Power of Vivid Color

You will find so many examples of this in daily life that not much needs to be said to convince you, I am sure, of the efficacy of color as an attention-grabber. You need only think of such things as red, blue, green, and yellow neon signs; pennants and banners in fluorescent reds and greens; and red, yellow, blue, green billboards.

Color photographs can help you call attention to a product and, with imagination, *even to an intangible* such as an investment. An investment sales pro who puts together and markets private offerings as diverse as shopping centers and cattle-feeding programs says she has used color photographs to give concrete expression to some of her projects. Clients know that the photos don't represent a program or a shopping center that is *now* being offered, but rather a *typical* offering.

A sign salesman walks up to "somebody in charge" and hands him or her a viewer which has full-color slides of several sign jobs put up by his company. This man could have complained that his company didn't furnish any colorful visual aids; instead he took a couple of rolls of 35 mm slides, bought an inexpensive slide viewer, and presto!—he had put the power of color to work.

Move Something—Move Anything

Your nervous system is almost totally without power to resist these attention-grabbers. Broad, or rapid, motion is a really compelling stimulus. It is almost magnetic in its drawing power, yet all but the real pros tend to overlook its effectiveness much of the time. And it can be as easy as moving some object "to provide a better view." If your demonstration has been rather static for awhile—with nothing but conversation going on—just a broad movement of the hand and arm, ostensibly to turn a catalog page, will help.

If you're making a group presentation, don't pace up and down: *Constant* motion loses its attention value, becomes boring. But when you need to call attention to some special point, try walking all the way around your display, your flip-charts, or whatever you're using.

Next, Try Selling with a Bang

This stimulus is virtually impossible to ignore, but it needs to be used with restraint to avoid irritating. A company selling electronic security devices (English translation: burglar alarms), equips each salesperson with a sample case rigged to provide a powerful, ear-splitting demonstration at the right moment.

LESSON NO. 24:
BALLYHOO

They're sometimes (but not often) called *barkers*. Carnival and circus show people more often call them *talkers, or openers*. They are *absolute masters* in the art of grabbing attention and holding on to it. On a carnival midway, the first opener or talker has the job of filling the sideshow tent for each performance, and he does this with a masterful combination of ballyhoo, raucous noise, dazzling color, and gyrating motion.

Never mind what you have seen in the movies. He doesn't stand there with a silly straw hat and a cane, saying "Tell you want I'm gonna do." What he *really* does is stand in silence on the "bally platform," waiting for the show across the midway to "turn the tip loose." With him on the platform are, perhaps, the fire-eater, the sword-swallower, the "frog man." As soon as the tip—or crowd—moves away from this competing show, the *talker* makes his move. He signals for somebody to start banging on a huge bass drum. Somebody else turns the amplifier on full. John Philip Sousa's "Stars and Stripes Forever" splits the night air, drowning out even the sound of the hurdy-gurdy on the merry-go-round.

As the tip moves across the midway, the talker signals for the fire-eater to blow a ball of blazing fluid into the air. The sword-swallower whirls a flashing blade, then catches it in his teeth. The talker holds the microphone close to his mouth and trills a vibrant, compelling "Hurrrryyyy—hurrrryyyy . . . ."

How to Move from Hoopla to Helpfulness

The old-time talker knew how to use the three master stimuli of color, motion, and noise in a manner which will perhaps never be equaled. Some would say that modern-day television commercials are a close second. Of course, they are entitled to this opinion. But I've never seen a *talker* you could walk out on, ignore, or turn off with a remote-control switch!

There are ways (and I'll cover them) to use much of the talker's psychological insights in your selling, and to put more pizazz and showmanship into your demonstrations. Modern professional salesmanship is somewhat more muted in its approach, but it needn't be *dead* because of that. The one thing that we have had to learn to keep on a professional level is that we must, from the very beginning, *involve* our clients in such a way that they feel that they are *part* of the "show"; that all the commotion involved in a demonstration is not something that is *happening* to them, but rather that they are full participants in what is taking place. It is not really difficult to do this; it's as easy as asking a question after each little "bit of business."

One manufacturer's rep uses a projector with its own screen, built into an attaché case. His factory furnishes an audiovisual strip which shows the product (a valve used in the petrochemical industry) being abused. This salesman says the film has a lot of flash, color, motion, and sound. But there are four *stopping points* in the ten-minute presentation. And at each of these points, he *involves* the client with questions like, "How would this affect your operation? Would a valve that had that kind of extra strength make a difference in the amount of downtime in your plant?" He could simply *say,* "Valves this tough would reduce the amount of downtime." But that wouldn't be *involvement.* It might, however, invite participation of a negative sort. Many clients, when not specifically *invited* to participate, will continually disrupt the demonstration, raising objection after objection simply to retain the feeling of being in control. You will probably find this to be especially true in this early stage of the sales process; the stage in which you are trying to secure the kind of *attention* that is strong enough to grip your prospects and to *hold* them long enough for you to really *interest* them in your proposition.

LESSON NO. 25:
THE QUESTION OPENER

You will not only ask questions to involve your prospects in such dramatic demonstrations as we have been talking about; you will learn in this lesson that the right kinds of questions can themselves have attention-grabbing power. Memorize some of these questions if you like. Or, after you study and analyze them, construct some of your own.

Ask an Innocent Question

What I'm calling the "innocent question" is not to be confused with the *inane* question! The innocent question is one that *truly is meant to elicit information,* albeit information that is not especially useful in a hard-boiled, pragmatic sense. For example, study this question:

"Are you the same Mr. Johnson who started this store fifteen years ago?"

When this kind of question is asked with just the right lilt in your voice, with just a hint of admiration (being careful not to overdo it), it is a terrific attention-getter. It is totally devoid of the imperious overtones accompanying such blunt questions as "Are you Mr. Johnson?" Here is another—this one with just a whisper of whimsy to it:

"Is it really true that you have the most complete stock in this part of town?"

Again, keep your voice light; ask the question with a smile on your face (and in your voice). Try your own variation of these questions; I know you will be pleased with the reaction you get. Now, just for comparison, let's look at an *inane* question:

"Is it hot enough for you?"

I can just imagine someone thinking "No, you yo-yo. I'd like for it to be twenty degrees hotter."

Another inane question (at least in a sales context) is this one:

"How's business?"

As totally useless as this question is, I have heard many salespeople ask it. There is one more question which many salespeople use—and which accomplishes about as much. Are you guilty of this one?

"How are you?"

Ask a Meaningful Question

While the *innocent* question seeks to arouse a feeling of benign well-being by eliciting information which seems to indicate that you are interested in the prospect, the *meaningful* question directs the prospect's attention to your proposition. This kind of question takes considerable thought and care to frame so that it will sound like a genuinely meaningful question—not an inane one! For example, you may have something which will actually cut your client's credit losses by 50 percent. You must be aware that there is likely to be a "credibility gap" in the early stages of your relationship, however. So move with caution. *Don't ask a ques-*

tion like, "If I could save you 50 percent on your credit losses, would you be interested?" That's an inane question. Here's how to ask the same question *meaningfully*:

> "Not everybody does as well, but Fred Bary over at Bary Hardware claims that he has cut his credit losses in half. Can you give me five minutes to tell you what he told me?"

The salesman who first showed me how to use this kind of question was selling a system of preprinted collection letters, and he says that before he learned how to ask questions in this manner, he had tried to qualify his prospect with a question such as this:

> "Do you have trouble with past-due accounts?"

To his surprise, few business people would admit to having any great difficulty from this source. Perhaps owning up to such difficulty was considered an admission of poor judgment, at least in the area of credit granting. However, when he simply *assumed* that everybody had such difficulties, then framed a question which suggested a solution to the assumed problem, the results were totally different!

Now, he claims, it is only the rare prospect who doesn't want to hear how "Fred Bary" cut his credit losses.

Other salespeople have made similar discoveries. Perhaps one more example will further clarify this point. Houston, Texas is often called the "Air-Conditioned City." This is so because it is extremely difficult to live there in the summertime without air conditioning, and it is virtually impossible to operate a business without it.

A woman selling a reflective plastic screen to Houston store owners says she *knows* how hot it gets there, so she doesn't have to ask about utility bills for cooling. She has discovered, too, that many people like to feel they are "on top of" things like cooling bills and would prefer not to admit to a stranger that they need help in controlling these costs. So she never asks if cooling costs seem high, etc. Instead, she uses this kind of question:

> "One of my customers says he has saved fifty dollars a month on his air conditioning costs for three months in a row. May I explain how he did it?"

She says that the usual response is something like, "What do you have?" Or, "Let me see what you have." Before she learned better, she was asking, "How would you like to save 20 percent on your electric bill?" And it didn't take her long to figure out that that was an inane question!

LESSON NO. 26:
OPEN WITH A FREE GIFT

"Sell" the Free Gift—Don't Give It Away

It sounds like a contradiction. But professional selling is not just a matter of exchanging goods or services for money. Professional selling means *adding value* to your goods or services so that your client will feel better about acquiring what you sell than he or she feels about the money exchanged for it. If you fail to add this value to what you offer, you will probably not sell it.

The intrinsic value of the free gift you are using as an attention-getter is of little consequence so long as the *perceived* value is relatively high. Some salespeople have learned how to raise this perceived value to an almost incredible extent. A brush salesman of my acquaintance knew more than a dozen ways to bend or "mold" a small give-away brush to make it more useful. The selfsame brush with a different bend in it was a vegetable brush or a pot scraper. With a squeeze and a twist, it became a denture brush. The brush cost him very little to buy, but (once he had "shaped" it) many customers tried to buy it from him. He would never sell it, however. After his little "sales talk" about the free brush, he would hand it over with a flourish, saying, "This is my free gift to you for being nice enough to stand here and listen to me."

It matters little what the free gift is. You can add tremendous value to it if you will simply take the time to think through several ways to use it. Never just *give* a gift to a client. *Demonstrate at least three uses or benefits*. The gift should draw its value not from its cost but from its unique quality of *usefulness*. It is up to you to discover and promote this usefulness.

Keep the Gift Simple

A gift should never be so ostentatious that it will be interpreted as an attempt to ingratiate oneself with the buyer (unless, of course, that is exactly what is intended). I would indeed be naive if I didn't know that, sometimes, sales *are* made this way. Although I have my own convictions in this regard, this is a book about selling—not about my moral code. I have been told too many times by sales pros that I trust: Some lines are so much like competitors' lines—point for point and price for price—that the thing that makes the sale might very well be the "perks" that go with the product.

I won't argue about this because I assume that this book is being read by adults who are capable of making "moral" decisions such as this for themselves. I can only say that if you are mistaken about the person to whom such a "gift" is offered, you may not only lose a potential customer but you may damage your own reputation. I was the buyer for a floor-covering operation several years ago when a salesman put two one hundred dollar bills on my desk. He had no way of knowing just what my authority was beyond my authority to buy his product. In other words, he couldn't know whether I would consider his "gift" as a *reduction* in the price of his product, which would be treated as a savings to my company, or whether I would consider the money as a personal gift. His comment removed all doubt about what he intended, however. He said "It's cash, so you don't have to tell anybody . . . ."

The sad part about this situation was that I was interested in this salesman's line as a lower-priced alternative to a similar product we were already stocking. Now I was afraid to buy—afraid that his product was far inferior to that which we were now stocking. Otherwise, why did he have to use such tactics? And did he have a reputation for making such offers—kickbacks—to other buyers in town? If he did, what would my employers think of me if they learned I'd bought from this man, however innocent the transaction had been?

Offer a Choice of Gifts

Whether you are using a low-cost gift or a more expensive one, keep the transaction businesslike. If your prospect can see a logical tie-in between your product and the gift, there is less likelihood that your gift giving will ever be suspect. It makes sense for the typewriter salesperson to give such gifts as machine covers, a special locking device that prevents easy theft or removal of the machine, or a carton of ribbons. It *doesn't* make sense (not the *same kind* of sense, anyhow) to give a case of whiskey or a gold cigarette case and lighter.

An easy way around a sometimes difficult situation is to offer a *choice*. This enables you to give a gift where such gifts prove helpful, but to do so in a manner which places the responsibility for acceptance on the buyer. One large mail-order office-supply firm offers an assortment of business and personal gifts which are pegged by a "point system" to definite purchase amounts. You can use a similar system yourself.

The "point system" works like this. The mail-order firm mentioned sends two catalogs to each customer. One catalog shows the merchandise, the prices and the amount of "points" that are given to the purchaser with each purchase. The second catalog shows the gifts that are available, and the "point cost" of each gift. With each sale, the customer is mailed a certificate showing the number of points he or she has coming for the sale. It is then up to the purchaser whether the certificates are redeemed for personal gifts or for business gifts. In fact, the mail-order firm has nothing to do with *redeeming* the certificates. The gift catalog and the gifts are handled by a sales promotion concern under contract. Your local specialty advertising firm can help you design such a program for your proposition, if you're interested.

If You Can't Keep It Simple, Keep It Timely

In my opinion, *all gifts* need to be tied, somehow, to the product or service you are selling: There needs to be a *reason* for the gift. There has to be a logical reason for giving a gift *instead* of a reduction in price. One method often used by top pros who understand the subtleties involved is this: Offer the gift as an *added inducement for acting today instead of later*. Prospects understand this kind of gift, react with attention and interest instead of suspicion.

LESSON NO. 27: MAKE A PROMISE

Promise a Future Benefit

The promise, *if it is believed,* is a powerful attention-getter. Or perhaps I should say if it is not *disbelieved.* The difference is subtle, but not trifling. Belief is very often a matter of the state of our *feelings* concerning some statement, condition, situation, or circumstance. Disbelief, on the other hand, is more often a matter of cold logic. You can believe in life after death simply because you have a powerful *feeling* that it is so. It has very little to do with logic. You may have this feeling about more mundane things as well; the belief—for example—that the earth is flat. We believe many things that we cannot prove, but *we tend to disbelieve everything we are able to disprove.*

The promise of a *future benefit* is made of the kind of stuff from which religious and political beliefs are made. And if you have learned to put the right kind of *feeling* in your voice as you make your promise, you needn't even stop to prove it. Just be sure that it cannot be disproved!

Here's one example of this principle at work, as it is used by a woman selling commercial real estate. She is talking to a prospective client about a tract of land on the edge of the city:

"I am excited about this proposition. You may be too, when you hear about it. I have discovered that the city has just started moving in this direction at a tremendous rate of speed. Somebody is going to get rich on this, and it could be you.''

Promise to Relieve Boredom

Your presentation should offer, at the very least, the promise of *entertainment*. Although things have changed a lot since the day of the old-time drummer with his stock of off-color jokes, don't make the mistake of thinking that professional selling means *dull* selling. It's true that some prospects have a natural tendency to be wary of strangers. It can be a bit more difficult to "entertain" them on the first visit. But there is absolutely no excuse for your prospects to still be avoiding you on the second or third visit. Make sure that each visit is pregnant with promise. Do things differently on subsequent visits. Change your "entrance." Have the nerve to do something drastic. Maybe carry your samples inside a cardboard box instead of in an attaché case. Or carry something in a paper bag. When you do something like this, you raise your prospect's level of expectancy. Your prospect *knows* what's in your attaché case by now. But what could you possibly have in that brown paper bag? Here are just five things you could do to raise the prospect's expectancy level and suggest the promise of entertainment—the relief of boredom. You can certainly think of many more.

1. Change your entrance.
2. Do something differently.
3. Change your appearance.
4. Change your tone of voice.
5. Go out and come back in.

Build Promise into Your Appearance

Your very bearing and demeanor should be fraught with promise. Remember that you stand absolutely no chance of interesting people until you have their *attention*. You have probably known people who seem to command attention by their very presence. Strive to become one of these people. Look at yourself in a full-length mirror. Don't be unkind now—this person is your best friend. But be honest: Is there something you can do *now* to create a more prepossessing image? Almost certainly there is. Do it.

Negative Promises Don't Sell

Pros rarely make this kind of mistake. But it does happen often enough to warrant at least a casual mention. Never say "This will take only a few minutes of your time." Some prospects interpret this to mean "I'll only bore you for a few minutes." There may be times when it seems wise to assure a new prospect that you will not take too long, but a more positive way of doing it is like this:

> "I promise not to take longer than three minutes, unless YOU ask me to."

This is really laying it on the line, but you will note that the promise is a far more positive one. Stick to your word if you use this one. Take your watch off and lay it in front of you. When your time is up, ask: "Do you want to hear more?" You've either aroused interest by now or you're wasting time.

LESSON NO. 28: SEX

Now That I Have Your Attention, What Do I Do Next?

Through the use of sex appeal it is easy to attract initial attention. The problem is, how do you transfer this attention to your product or service? The people on Madison Avenue have worked on this one for years with a great deal of success, as long as we are talking about selling via television and the various print media. *Personal selling,* however, is another matter.

Sex Appeal and The Trade-Show Booth

A source of leads exploited with marked success by many kinds of firms is the trade show. Really attractive people with the right personality are invaluable as booth attendants, especially when it comes to getting trade-show visitors to register for drawings, prizes, etc. A truly vital person with verve and flash can get a person of the opposite sex to fill out those forms and drop them in the box, and no amount of point-of-purchase advertising can do it nearly so well.

The Sexy Telephone Voice

No amount of writing can describe what a sexy voice sounds like. Probably nobody needs to read such a description anyhow. About the only thing that needs to be said about it is that when you have such a voice, people of the opposite sex seem generally more interested in what you have to say—they like the sound of your voice and will often listen longer without interruption than they would otherwise. If you have such a voice—enjoy. If you don't, I doubt that you can fake it. It would probably sound like an obscene call.

Should a Buyer Ever Be "Fixed Up"?

Again, I would like to avoid any discussion of any possible "moral" issue. I'm going to continue in the assumption that you want to know what top pros feel and do about this. I have known and talked to many on this subject. Most of them say that they would not do this. I must say in all honesty, however, that a substantial minority see nothing wrong in this practice.

"Fixing a buyer up with a hot number is just smart business," one oil-tool salesman told me. "Especially foreign buyers. If you don't do it, your competition sure as hell will," he insisted.

I have never discussed this in any of the many articles I've written on selling; I feel uneasy about it now. Perhaps it is more a commentary on the *times* than it is on the profession of selling to say that the practice seems to be growing.

Sex Appeal and Personal Magnetism

Sex appeal needn't have anything to do with illicit sex; it more often does not. Perhaps a better name for it is *personal magnetism*. It is more apparent in cross-gender relationships, but this dynamic spark of personal power and attraction can just as easily exist between two completely heterosexual persons of the same sex. It is simply an energy—a life force—that seems to drive top professionals to seek out the company of other human beings, even when they aren't selling.

When you have a large measure of this personal power *all* facets of your life (not just your sex life) seem to operate more smoothly, more efficiently, more harmoniously. *Elan vital* is the name given to this energy in Bergsonian philosophy, in which it is seen as the original vital impulse which is the substance of both consciousness and nature!

LESSON NO. 29: ATTRACT ATTENTION WITH AN OUTSTANDING FEATURE

What Makes Your Product or Service Unique?

There is probably at least one truly outstanding feature which your product or service has and which makes it stand out above its competitors. For the purpose of attracting attention, build a "minitalk" on this one feature and its corresponding benefit. If you sell something that has many similar competitors, you may have to dig to find this special feature. Don't give up. Remember that the special feature/benefit you are looking for may not even be one which you or your company considers especially important. The important thing is that it should be a feature and benefit combination that none of your competitors are stressing (whether they have it or not).

For example, two insurance companies were bidding on a sizable group policy for a printing firm which employed several hundred persons. The *terms and conditions* of the policies were identical, since the specifications had been laid out in advance, and both insurance companies were required to bid on exactly those "specs." The premium rates bid by the two insurance companies were within a few cents of each other—and this on a premium of more than $20,000 per month! But one of the companies had a local claims-payment office, while the other did not. The sales rep didn't talk about anything else. He hammered home the fact that his company was the one in a position to make immediate settlement of any claims. He stressed the speed and dispatch which could be effected only by a local claims-payment office. He talked about letters that get lost in the mail. He talked about the red tape involved in writing to an out-of-town payment center. Over and over, like a broken phonograph record, he said it: local claims payments . . . local claims payments . . . local claims payments.

When the time came for the trustees for the printing company and its union to make the buying decision, it was almost a foregone conclusion. The insurance company with the local claims-payment office got the business.

In your search for the truly unique features of your proposition, don't overlook one most important feature which no competitor can possibly offer: *you*. Of course, what you need to concern yourself about at this point is *how to make your specialness obvious*. Remember, at this stage in the selling process (the attention-getting stage) we are not trying to *prove*, we are trying to *impress*. And remember, too, that every one of your competitors has somebody who can also say, "None of my competitors has *me*."

So how do you do that? How do you make your *specialness* obvious? Here are some things to think about that may bring you just a bit closer to understanding what makes you special. And when you understand that, you are in a much better position to "sell" this specialness to others.

1. Think about yourself. You *are* special, aren't you? You have special talents and abilities which you can talk about. With just a bit more enthusiasm you can make your specialness obvious. Say to yourself several times a day, "I am excited about me!"
2. Think about your prospect. Think in terms of what your specialness means to this person. List at least five ways in which only *you* can benefit your prospect at this time and in this place.
3. Think about what made your employer pick you over other job applicants. You don't know why he did this? *You don't know?* Find out. Ask.
4. Think about what you are prepared to do for your clients that most salespeople would not do.
5. Pretend that you are going to furnish material for a brochure that will be written about you.
6. Make notes as you go through this list. When you are done, write the material for such a brochure as described in "5," above.

There are other things that you can do to enhance your own awareness of your specialness. At some time or another during your career, you may have written a resume to present to a prospective employer. In many larger cities there are professional resume writers who do this kind of work for a fee. Of course, some of these "writers" are simply good typists and have only the ability to neatly type what you write out. And that's okay, if that's what you want. But just remember, this is not *writing;* this is *typing*. Unfortunately, they don't call themselves *resume typists*, but *resume writers*.

If you are lucky enough (or astute enough) to spot a good *writer* of resumes, you should expect to pay a fee that is on a par with that charged by other professionals. The product turned out by this kind of a pro will be well worth the fee. Now, why am I spending all this time talking about resumes and resume writers? Well, let me say that it's not to suggest that you need a resume to help you find another job. But I have written scores of resumes for persons looking for work, and here is an interesting discovery that I have made. I have never knowingly lied or exaggerated on a resume, but I *have* taken care that *the truth I tell is done in an interesting and effective manner*. I believe that the resumes I have written have had a truly-telling effect on the persons they were intended to impress. But here is what I discovered: The *subjects* of my resumes have always told me that they were much more impressed with *their own abilities* after they had read what I had written!

However, before you dash out to find a resume writer, there is just one more word of warning I would like to give you. Never hire such a writer until you have had the opportunity to study samples of his or her work. Some such writers are not exceptionally good writers, but are (alas!) terrific salespeople!

Just one more word about resume writers before we move on.

You may feel up to writing your own resume. I strongly urge that you try this before you hire someone to do it. Remember my warning about *writers* who are better salespeople than they are writers. A mass-produced, stereotyped document would not only fail as a resume, but would not do much to make you feel better about yourself either. There are several good books out that can help you to write your own resume. Some of these books can give you much helpful advice on career growth and development as well. One of the best of these is *What Color Is Your Parachute?*, by Richard Bolles (Ten Speed Press).

Most of these "career guidance" books assume that you are looking for a job, and in a very real sense you are. A salesperson starts several *new jobs*, with *new employers* every week. Each prospect you meet is a prospective new employer. Many of the suggestions contained in these books will help you to analyze your *job finding* (read "prospecting") technique, and will show you how to improve it. I can only hint at the wealth of other information that these books can give you. Bolles' *What Color Is Your Parachute?* has a book list and resource list that is alone worth the price of the book.

Personalize Your Service Department

Everybody talks about what great service they give, so you're not going to get a lot of favorable attention by making an unsupported claim that you give better service. If it is true that you firm gives better service, your client will learn this over time. However, what you need to do is to convince the client *ahead of time* that your service department is something special. How do you do this? *You build a case* for your service people. If you don't know these people personally, get to know them—on a first-name basis. Get some pictures of your service people and of the service department. Get some service *anecdotes,* some stories you can tell about how Joe Brown or Mary Smith handled this or that difficult service problem.

A computer salesman uses this technique to great advantage. He emphasizes the technical expertise of his service department (actually, a one-man "department" operated by his employer, an electronics genius). This salesman has several service stories that he can pick from, but he gets a lot of mileage from one story which tells how his employer saved the day by "inventing" a miniature computer to demonstrate a data-entry device that he was selling. He has learned to tell "service stories" so well that they have become an integral part of his sales presentation. With practice, you can do the same thing. Begin by using these stories to attract initial favorable attention. Soon they will become second nature to you, and you will find yourself dropping them here and there in your presentation.

LESSON NO. 30: HOW TO USE THE "TWO-BY-FOUR" OPENER

First, You Have To Get a Mule's Attention

You have probably heard the story about the farmer who had just bought a mule. When he tried to get the mule to leave with him, the mule wouldn't budge. It made no difference whether he called the mule's name, tugged at the rope, or yelled; the result was the same. The mule's former owner picked up a piece of fence post (a "two-by-four") and whacked the mule across the head. "One thing you have to learn about mules," he said, "is that you first have to get their attention."

You will not attract the right kind of attention by just being "nice" to people. Some of your prospects are past masters at being "nice," and some of them can "nice" you right out the door before you know what's happened. You have probably discovered this for yourself; perhaps you need to be reminded of it.

While you certainly would not want to take such drastic measures as the farmer with the mule, there will be times when you will need to do something drastic. The "two-calls-in-one-day" approach is such a drastic measure, and it sometimes gets attention when nothing else does. It is the essence of simplicity. You just do what the name implies.

I know that you have had it happen that you did all of the things you usually do to get favorable attention, and nothing happened. I mean nothing. There were no questions, no objections; no interaction of any kind. You might be wrong to consider this kind of situation a turndown. In all likelihood, your prospect was so terribly preoccupied (perhaps with a serious personal problem) that you couldn't get through. If you suspect that this is what has happened, try this. Leave as graciously as you can and come back later in the day. On your next call you might say something like, "You know, I forgot something very important when I was here earlier." Then go through your presentation again.

The chances are, if you have correctly assessed your prospect as having a bad case of "preoccupitis," he or she will not even remember having heard the material before! Even so, the worst thing that could happen is that you would be reminded that you had already been over it.

When There's "Nothing" to Be Thankful for, Write a Note

I have written a number of articles for *Specialty Salesman Magazine* (now named *Selling Direct*). In one article (which was titled "Thank You For Nothing"), I told about a salesman who sold sign-making kits and who had heard a complaint from a prospective customer concerning the reputation of the product that he was selling. The stick-on letters, this prospect had heard from a user in the neighborhood, did not stick. Many salespeople, when confronted with this kind of objection, would argue or simply ignore it. Not this salesman. He investigated and found that the complaint was well founded, even though it was the customer's fault; he had used the kit to make a *permanent* sign, rather than a temporary sign like a "Sale" sign. This salesman quickly perceived that a good product was about to get a bad reputation. He not only told his customer how to avoid the difficulty in the future, but now he warns new purchasers that, if they want to make "permanent" signs, they have to add a drop of glue to the letters. And he even started giving a small tube of glue to every purchaser for this purpose.

But this salesperson did something else, something *special*. He sat down and wrote a thank-you note to the man who had told him of the problem. And, because of the reaction he got, because of the pure *attention value* of this note, he now looks for excuses to write notes!

Get the note-writing *habit*. This one thing is so unexpected, so unusual a thing for a salesperson to do that it instantly grabs the kind of attention that lasts—and ripens into deep interest; interest not only in your proposition, but in YOU.

Sales trainer John Wolfe is another one who knows the value of these brief notes. John is a tremendously successful person. He is the author of *Sell Like An Ace, Live Like A King,* and of other works. In a feature article I wrote for the *Houston Business Journal,* I used something like a printed page to describe some of John's sales-training methods. He really didn't *need* the "free press" which he got from the article. Yet, about a week after the article appeared, I got a note from John. This is what the note said:

> I just read the feature article you wrote on sales trainers. You did a super job. Sharp!

Now, I've been writing for enough years that I didn't need the kind of ego boost a note like this can give you. But just the fact that an obviously busy person would take the time to write such a note is meaningful. I felt like writing him a letter thanking him for his thank-you note.

LESSON NO. 31: HOW TO USE THE NAME-DROPPER OPENER

Joe Sent Me

It's an old one, and it conjures up visions of one-way mirrors and underworld hoodlums peeking through peepholes. But it's a fact: There is nothing more attention-compelling than the name of a friend, dropped at the right time. If you can honestly tell your prospect that a friend of his or hers "sent" you—or even suggested that you call—you have gone a long way toward getting favorable attention. It needn't even be a really close friend; even the name of an acquaintance helps to avoid that coldness and suspicion that usually comes with the typical confrontation of strangers.

Drop the Name of Mr. Big

While any familiar name can help to break the ice, the name of some person who is considered a leader can have a special effect. There is a special way of using Mr. Big's name that can make an important difference in its value as an attention-getter. You'll need to be careful, first of all, that you don't make an issue of the fact that Mr. Big is your customer—just drop the name casually. Your prospect may admire Mr. Big's success, but it may be a *grudging* sort of admiration.

Don't overlook the fact that your prospect may also be somebody else's Mr. Big. If you discover that this is so, be quick to drop the name of that person, pointing out that your prospect is held in high esteem.

Keep Adding Names to Your "Drop List"

Most of the names on your "drop list" will be customers of yours. They needn't be customers to be effective, if you do it right. If you learn that some important people are using a service like yours, you can drop these names, too. I once knew a salesman who made a good living selling subscriptions to a religious magazine. A portion of the subscription price went to support poor students who were studying for the ministry. This salesman would start working in a new territory by having everybody he called on write their name on a sheet of paper headed *Honor Roll,* "just to show I made the call." After he had four or five names, he would bring the *Honor Roll* out at the beginning of his presentation. He wouldn't say anything about the names, but there was the implication that they had already bought. As he made sales, he added these new names to his "Honor Roll." Within a couple of hours he had a sizable list of names to drop. Of course, I dislike anything that is less than totally honest, as I am sure you do. I only mention this saleman's tactics to show the power of name dropping.

Ask for Names to Add to Your Drop List

Although professionalism today demands a far greater degree of integrity than that which was required in the day of the old-time magazine salesman, there are still quite *legitimate* ways of using the principle he used. For more on this, read "Thumbnail Testimonials" in Lesson No. 45. In that lesson you will learn about a system of referral letters ("notes" would be a better description) which your prospect can read in a hurry. What I'm suggesting here is that, once you have collected a batch of referrals, or testimonials, that you make a *list* of the names of these people (your "Honor Roll"), which you can simply leave in plain view as you launch your presentation. Just a brief mention that you have letters (or notes) from each of the people whose names are on your list, and a slight tap of the list to call attention to it, can be very effective.

LESSON NO. 32:
USE ENTHUSIASM TO GET ATTENTION

Enthusiasm Is More Convincing When It Builds

The kind of enthusiasm that works is the *believable* kind. Don't come on too strong, especially if it is your first call on a prospect. Just remember, *nobody believes you're all that glad to see them if they don't know you.*

People you have called on for some time can accept you as an energetic, enthusiastic person. They won't keep looking for your "angle."

Beginning salespeople make this mistake often. They try too hard, try to get too much *bubble* in their voices. Frequently, they come across as affected, phony. This won't likely happen to you *if you really are enthusiastic*. Neither will it happen if you are a long-time *professional*, who has really learned the art of playing the part like a professional actor does. However, feigning enthusiasm (or any other emotion) when you don't know what you're doing can be disastrous. You are sure to come across like an "actor" in a school play; and that's a different sort of actor—and a different sort of performance!.

Learn "The Method" First

Before you can use the power of enthusiasm as an attention-getter, you will need to work on yourself first—to be sure that you have a good understanding of how to project enthusiasm. To do this effectively you will need to feel it; either naturally or by using the techniques of the school of acting known as *Method acting*. As actor using Method techniques can cry or laugh at will, for example. Notice I didn't say *pretend* to be crying or laughing. In brief, here is the Method.

Sit alone, and think sad thoughts. If you need to, see someone you love in trouble—bad trouble. Or see him or her dead. Or imagine yourself (that's someone you love, isn't it?) in terrible distress. Keep it up until tears come to your eyes, if you can. Next try to do the opposite; picture a happy scene, for your loved ones and for yourself. Try to laugh. (Turn your tape recorder on to check yourself on this later.) Keep at it until the laugh is genuine.

As you perform these practices, try to capture the *feeling tone* which you have generated by your imagining. Once you can summon up this feeling without having to form the images (sad pictures, happy scenes, etc.), you've got it made!

You Will Laugh All the Way to the Bank

As far as selling is concerned, there is not too much reason for you to learn how to cry on demand. But laughing is something else. *Enthusiasm goes with laughter*. It makes a lot of sense to learn how to laugh, not just when you hear a joke or watch a funny movie, but to laugh just for the fun of laughing. Of course, the ability to laugh at a joke which your customer tells you (even when it's not funny) can mean money in the bank for you. I'm not talking about the usual polite chuckle, I'm talking about real laughter! You can't *fake* laughter, it will sound fake. But you can *learn* to laugh "on demand" with practice and by actually placing the demand on yourself. Again, get off by yourself, and start laughing out loud. You will be a bit self-conscious at first, but keep at it anyhow. Very soon you will be laughing at yourself. If you practice often enough, you will learn how to do it.

There are many fringe benefits to being able to laugh easily. You will feel great after a good laugh. Look up some of the references to laughter in any good book of quotations. *Reader's Digest* has a department called "Laughter Is The Best Medicine." The writer Norman Cousins cured himself of a supposedly terminal illness by laughing regularly, *several times a day*. Laughing often, and energetically, can make you an enthusiastic person.

3

The Customer
Comes First

It's a fact that every sales manager and every book on selling keep trying to pound home: No matter how scintillating is your personality, your customers don't care about *you*. And no matter how wonderful is your product or service, *they don't care about that, either*. What they care about is *their family, their business, their problems*. You and what you sell are important only in relation to these customer concerns. It may sound like an old saw, but it is the groundwork upon which you must build your successful professional career. No matter how important your personal concerns seem to you, this one central fact is what it's all about. In each sales transaction you must convince your customer that you live by this dictum: *The customer comes first*.

LESSON NO. 33:
BENEFIT, BENEFIT, BENEFIT

How Do You Know What Your Prospects Want?

You may know your proposition so well that you can recite the facts about it in your sleep. You *should* know them that well. But you must be aware that your prospect will consider this wonderful store of knowledge to be completely useless, unless somewhere, tucked inside of all that knowledge, is the answer to a specific problem or concern. In short, you have to give them what they want. But how do you give them what they want if you don't know what it is? How can you, a stranger, be expected to know what a prospect's problems are? Can you just ask? Try it sometime. Just walk up to a stranger and ask: "What problems of yours would you like to have me solve?"

Ridiculous? Absolutely! Presumptuous? Of course! Yet it is this very presumption that prospects face every time a salesperson walks in cold and starts talking about the features of a product or service.

Forget Your Product's Features

There is no feature of your product or service that is truly interesting to your prospect. No feature of your product can truly satisfy a deep-felt need. Believe it, for it is true. You have the fastest delivery in town? Your prospect doesn't want *anything* delivered unless such delivery solves a pressing need. The business of talking about your proposition only in terms of your client's needs is a complex one. You might easily fall in love, for example, with a piece of high-tech equipment. That may also happen to your *customer* once the sale has been made. But never forget that the purchase needs to be justified on the basis of satisfaction of some perceived need. Here is a mnemonic device (a memory peg) that will help you. Let's call this memory aid "the four *I*'s": *Identify, Isolate, Intensify,* and *Interpret.*

1. *Identify.* You cannot satisfy a client's need if you don't know what it is. Yet, your prospective client may attempt to keep you from learning what his or her needs are. You can learn what they are if you will take the time to establish credibility with your prospective client. Sometimes this will not happen until the second or third (or fourth) call. Hang in there. Persist. People don't like to share family secrets with strangers. If you call long enough to become a friend, things will change. You will identify the relevant needs.

2. *Isolate.* Once you are accepted and trusted, you may find yourself facing a cluster of client needs. You will identify at least one, more likely several areas in which you can be of service. If you are new at selling, the temptation may be great to come on like an expert in too many areas at once. It is better to establish your credibility by *isolating* one pressing need which you are *sure you can fill.* Take a fresh look at your proposition, and see *how many ways it can satisfy this one pressing need.* This could easily mean that you will have to develop *several* complete demonstrations; one for each need that you encounter frequently.

3. *Intensity.* Once you have determined which need you are going to address, you should do everything you are capable of doing to show your client that this need is important enough to demand immediate satisfaction. This is a point that many salespeople miss. A client may even tell you about certain needs, yet will not *feel* the need strongly enough so that the need is *uncomfortable. You must make your client painfully aware of a perceived need before he or she will act on that need.*

4. *Interpret.* You are an *interpreter.* You should never get involved in describing the intricacies of a proposition without showing how each new complication in the proposition corresponds with some intense need of your client and how it will assuage the feeling of discomfort associated with that need. In doing this, there will be times that you need only say it is so. At other times, the *words* you use may lack the power to carry your meaning; you will need to be careful of your intonation and your gestures.

LESSON NO. 34:
THE ART OF ACTIVE LISTENING

Listen with a Notepad

Nothing flatters a person more than having someone show respect by listening. More than that, however, *active listening* gives you special insights into a prospect's or client's thinking processes that are invaluable to *you*. A notepad can be a tremendous aid to the listening process. Be careful, however, that your attention remains riveted on the speaker—not on your notes. Maintain eye contact as much as possible, while capturing the essence of your client's comments on paper. Watch for natural pauses in your client's flow of words, and jump in every so often by saying, "May I ask you a question?" Then go back to something you have made a note about, and ask for amplification.

Words—Road Maps to Your Prospect's Mind

Pay special attention to the *words* your prospect uses. If any are not a part of your functional vocabulary (whether you *understand* them or not), write them down. At the first opportunity, ask a question like: "You used the word *bojack*. Does this refer to a trade-in which has little value, but which you accepted simply to make a sale on one of your higher-priced units?" (A "bojack" is just such a trade-in accepted by vacuum cleaner salespeople.) Many such terms can give you special insight, not only into the individual client's thinking, but into the way much of the industry itself looks at certain details of its business.

Used car dealers, for instance, use such terms as "drives out good" to describe a fairly good used car; one at least good enough to stand test-driving by potential buyers. Another frequently used term is "will run out the notes," meaning a car that should last at least until it's paid for.

Participate Physically in the Conversation

Head nodding and chair-edge hanging are two highly recommended practices. You probably understand this instinctively. What you may not realize, however, is that such participative listening has definite *reinforcement* value. Let me explain. Listen carefully to what your prospect is saying. Nod your head vigorously when the prospect says something that indicates a movement in the direction of making a purchase—even if it is only a slight movement in that direction. The merest expression of interest should be so rewarded. On the other hand, when the prospect says anything *negative,* that is anything that indicates a movement away from your proposition, be completely immobile. Don't frown or scowl—above all, don't argue. Watch how the prospect will tend to seek out those reinforcing nods! Studies in the field of social psychology bear out the validity of this statement.

Be Interested in Them and
They Will Be Interested in You

I don't agree with those sales trainers who imply that you should be willing to listen to your client totally without interruption—no matter what the subject of the monolog is. It is because of this disagreement that I suggest that you learn the art of "active" listening. You really don't convince people that you are interested in them by letting them ramble. Sooner or later you will discover this truth on your own: Many prospects ramble simply because they are trying desperately to find some area of agreement. They are trying to get · *reinforcement* from you for something—anything—they have done or said. So strong is this need in some people that they will keep talking—seemingly without purpose—until they get it! Give them what they want, and they will try to give you what you want.

Here's another reason why you can't just let them ramble. Many people who do this don't even look at you when they talk. Often they will look all around you and only glance at you once in a while. It is almost as though they are afraid that you will express some disapproval. If this is the case, then you absolutely *must interrupt in order to give them the kind of positive feedback they are trying so hard to get!* Just remember what we said earlier about reinforcing those comments which suggested a movement *toward* your proposition and ignoring those comments which represented a movement *away* from it. By doing this *you* retain control even when the prospect is talking! Yet you do this in a manner which indicates interest in what is being said.

LESSON NO. 35:
INTERACTIVE TALKING

Feed Forward and Feed Back

Use a sixty-second checkup to see if you're on target. You should rarely talk for more than a minute without getting feedback, at least during the early stages of your presentation. This means that you will have to pack these one-minute segments with words of power and strength. See Lesson No. 36 for help in doing this. It should be obvious to you that if you are going to keep your sales talk short (or at least keep each "burst" short), you will have to know your material so well that you never fumble for words. This doesn't necessarily mean delivering a memorized talk, but it does mean delivering a *learned* talk—one that you know well enough that you can deliver it with confidence, poise, and dispatch. And it also means that you will have to establish that *you are in charge of the sales interview*! Here's how you stay in charge while being sure that you are on target: Each time you deliver a "burst" of selling fire, end on a note of authority, then ask a question. Here's an example:

"Mr. Johnson, anyone wearing one of your advertising T-shirts is like a walking billboard. You couldn't *pay* that person to carry a sign or to wear a 'sandwich board' for you. Yet, for some reason, people will not only wear your advertising without charge, they will even *buy* these T-shirts from you. In effect, *they will pay you for advertising for you*! What would it do for your budget if your regular employees paid you for the privilege of working for you?"

Leave Plenty of Holes for Questions

The secret to interactive talking lies in the fact that you always leave plenty of "holes" in your presentation so that your client or prospect can participate, but participate *only* along the lines which you have planned. This is vitally important.

The Question That Doesn't Sound Like a Question

When you ask a question, it sounds like a question. When your prospect asks a question, it often sounds like a statement. This is because the client or prospect often asks questions which are couched in the form of *objections*. For example, you may have just presented a short burst of selling talk like this:

"This kind of investment is obviously not for everybody. It certainly isn't for the type of person who is still worried about finding enough money to take care of his or her family's current needs. But for the professional person like yourself who can afford to take the kind of risks involved in earning *big profits,* a private offering like this can make the difference between being comfortable and being wealthy. In just five years it could make the difference between luxury and opulence. Let me ask you just one question. If I can show you evidence that would convince you at least of the possibilities in this kind of investment, can you comfortably afford the $100,000 investment required?"

Now you have asked a question. You know it is a question, the prospect recognizes it as a question. But your prospect comes back with something like this:

"I suppose I could afford it. But I'm accustomed to making investments with more assurance of profit, even though smaller and with less risk. . . . "

That sounded like a statement, didn't it? If you accept it as a statement instead of a question, you will be trapped by your own definition of what a question is. Never mind the grammatical definition of a question; a question does not *always* end with a question mark—neither does it always end in a rising tone of voice. These are the characteristics of the grammatical construction known as the *interrogatory sentence*. For our purposes a question is simply a request for more information, no matter how that request is phrased.

"Let Me See if I Can Answer That Question for You"

This is the magic phrase that shows your prospect that what he or she thought was an objection was, in fact, simply a request for more information. The truly magical thing about it is that the prospect will always permit you to continue talking—if for no other reason than to hear the "answer to the question"! Want more magic? *You needn't even address yourself to the material contained in the objection.* So long as your presentation continues to be interesting, you can usually delay your "answer" until *you feel* the time is right.

LESSON NO. 36:
IN THE BEGINNING WAS THE WORD

Strong Words Put Power in Your Presentation

Selling is more than talking; an effective demonstration is probably more powerful than the best "sales talk" ever delivered. But the fact remains that the spoken word is still charged with carrying most of the freight in perhaps the majority of everyday circumstances. And there are times when, no matter how elaborate a presentation you are carrying in your case, some prospects won't even let you open the case unless you *sell* them on the idea first. There are times when *words* are still your best friend! But some words sell better than others. Some words that mean the same thing carry a different "load" of meaning. How can you tell *which* words do the best job for you? Well, regardless of what you can say in favor of the spontaneity you feel when you simply "wing" it, the prepared presentation gives you the opportunity to test different words. People who write advertising copy often test the copy for effectiveness by changing one word at a time. You can do the same thing, but to do this you must *know* what words you are using. You can't do this in "off the cuff" presentations.

Try Patches of Purple

There are many emotion-bearing words that can effectively tie your prospects' interests to your product's benefits. Salespeople who have learned the value of a good story usually understand how to use these "patches of purple," these words that draw vivid pictures by enlisting the clients' emotions. I know one such salesperson who never simply *tells* a story about someone using his product, he paints a word-picture. He sells water pumps to buyers in the oil fields in Texas. The kind of language he uses might well seem without "class" to tender ears, but his annual sales volume shows that he knows what he is doing.

"Some of my competitors are young engineers right out of college. They call on people in the oil patch wearing a business suit and their Sunday manners. Sales engineers, they call themselves. Hey—I don't knock it. Everybody's got to make a living. But I tell my customers that I know that what they really care about is *awl*—oil. And I tell 'em I'm the guy on duty twenty-four hours a day if they need me. They can get my ass out of bed at two A.M. if one of my pumps breaks down. When they buy or rent one of my pumps *I go with it*. Maybe they don't get *finesse* when they buy from me—but they don't get b.s., either! No finesse and no b.s., that's my motto," he says.

Admittedly, this kind of verbal rough and tumble will not work for many (perhaps most) sales propositions and most salespeople. The point is that you should understand how to splash your canvas with these bold swaths of color whenever and wherever you can. And if you discover that your *client* talks this way, believe me—sooner or later you will have to learn to relate in this fashion. There are, however, other ways of using boldness and color in your choice of words *without* sounding like a roustabout. Undoubtedly this kind of color will be more appropriate 90 percent of the time.

Meet Mr. Webster, Mr. Roget, and Mr. Rodale

Using words effectively doesn't mean using "big" words. There is absolutely no point in using a word that sends your client scurrying to the dictionary. However, for every ordinary word you now use, there are at least four or five other words that mean *almost* the same thing.

One of the best synonym books that I have found is *The Synonym Finder*, by J.I. Rodale (Rodale Press, Emmaus, Pa.). A companion to this book is another Rodale book, called *The Word Finder*. You will find ways of *combining* words that would never have occurred to your mind unaided. I can't begin to describe the richness of this book in the short space of this lesson, but here's a hint. Most of the words we use in speaking stand naked and bare. Adjectives are usually weak and watery. Rarely is a "strong" thing more than "*very* strong." Look up "strong" in Rodale's *Word Finder*. You will find a list of almost thirty adverbs which can modify the word *strong*. Here is a veritable palette of adverbs; words such as *brutally, physically, powerfully, vigorously*—any many more words which paint a picture of just *how* strong.

While you're at it, be sure that you have a copy of *Roget's Thesaurus*, and get yourself a good dictionary. There are several occupations in which words are the stock in trade. Law is such an occupation. So is writing. And so is *professional selling*. Don't let *your* stock run down.

LESSON NO. 37: DISTRACTIONS, AND HOW TO HANDLE THEM

Understand Your Client's Environment

Bear in mind that what you consider distracting may very well be a necessary *part* of what your client does for a living. If your customer is, say, the general foreman of a large machine shop, you should *expect* that many of your presentations will be made against a background of burrs, whines, and scrapes. It is true that the Occupational Safety and Health Act (OSHA) has mandated that the level of noise be reduced by many decibels. People who work in such shops can appreciate such a difference. If it's your first time in such an environment as a machine shop or a large print shop, you will likely still find the noise unbearable at first. Sometimes there is nothing you can do but learn to get used to it. A better approach, however, is to come to *understand* your customer's environment.

When you come to understand the industrial environment, you learn about such things as *shift changes, downtime, waiting time*. During these gaps in the work routine you will often be able to talk to the industrial buyer without distractions.

There are other kinds of distractions you will need to overcome, too. Remember that business—the *kind of business* your client has opened the doors to pursue—goes on even though it might seem to your advantage for it to stop. This normal work flow may seem like an interruption to you; rarely is it so to your client, and the more thoroughly you understand this the better will be your ability to cope. A customer walks up while you are in the middle of your presentation. What do you do? I have two suggestions: (1) If this seems like an isolated occurrence, smile and say in a pleasantly low tone of voice, "Take care of your customer." If it keeps happening, you probably have come at the wrong time. (2) If it is apparent that the time is wrong, say so: "I'm sorry. I can see that you're doing your best to listen to me, but you have other important things to tend to. When would be a better time for me to come back?" It is very difficult for your prospect to refuse an appointment for a later time if it is handled in this manner.

Learn the Power of Total Concentration

You probably have discovered that it is not so much your *client* who is distracted by interruptions; it is more often *you* who are so distracted. Many buyers have reached a high level of professionalism in the operational aspects of their business. Most have the ability to juggle several problems at the same time. Frequently, they can add an additional level of complication—*you*—with the ease born of long practice. If your presentation is so well organized that you can pick up without difficulty whenever you are interrupted, you should be able to work with whatever distractions come up. A tremendous help in doing this is what I call *total concentration.*

Concentration can be learned by practice. In fact, that is the only way it can be learned. No matter how well I explain how you concentrate, when I have finished explaining it you still will not concentrate any better. It's like playing the piano. You simply have to *determine* that you will do it and then practice diligently. Perhaps you will improve if you study as well as practice. But here is the important point: Many people have learned to play the piano simply by sitting down to play and by repeating this procedure every day. In short, they have learned to play by *playing*. Probably *not one person has ever learned to play the piano by only studying how to play the piano.* There is something built into the human system which permits one to pick out "by ear" the correct sequence of notes which make up a musical melody. This ability won't manifest itself the first time for most people, but with patience and persistence it usually will.

It is much the same with learning to concentrate. The pattern is there, waiting to be called forth. Place the demand on yourself, and you will eventually be rewarded with an increased ability to work your way through the most distracting of distractions!

LESSON NO. 38: SIX MAGIC WORDS
THAT LEAD TO PROSPECT INTEREST

Probably you have run across these six words in another context. These are actually one-word questions that everybody likes to have answered about any new situation or condition. Newspaper writers are cautioned to make sure that every story answers the first four of these "questions": Who? What? When? Where? It has been my experience that most people are also curious about "how" and "why" most of the time. Consider the importance of these words in your sales presentation.

1. *Who* will benefit from this transaction? Remember, if only one party benefits it's not a sale at all—it's a gift . . . or a theft. Your clients and prospects may not ask you, but they always want to know *who* else in the industry is already using your product or service. The *who else* question is important to you, too. You should early form the habit of asking your client, *"Who else do you know who would be interested?"*

2. *What* your product will do is more important than what it is, but your client wants to know both of these things right at the beginning of your presentation. Sometimes it is smart selling to talk about *what* the product will do at some length before going into the details of what the product is. The "what is it" or curiosity factor can be a powerful interest holder, if it is handled right. I know a vacuum cleaner salesman who tells prospects, "I wouldn't waste your time trying to sell you a vacuum cleaner." What he sells is a "complete home sanitation system." He explains what the health benefits of his system are, using charts, drawings, statistical and documentary evidence. When the prospect is thoroughly saturated with *what* the product will do, then (and only then) will he get his machine out of the car.

3. *When* does a purchasing decision need to be made? It is usually to your advantage that the purchase be made *now!* It probably comes as no surprise to you that your prospect (even when convinced of the need) often does not feel this same urgency. This is a point that many beginners overlook: You can make a truly convincing and powerful presentation which absolutely convinces the prospect of a need for your product, yet leave with nothing in your orderbook. You must answer this question for your client: "When do I have to buy this product or service in order to get these benefits? Is there any reason why I can't wait until tomorrow?"

Very few purchasing decisions absolutely must be made *today,* and your customers know this. It is true that the customer doesn't have to *buy* now, but you must *sell* now! Now is the only time you *can* sell. If you're smart, you will figure out several reasons why it will be more advantageous for your prospect to become a customer today rather than tomorrow . . . or next week . . . or. . . . *You* need to answer the question *"when."* Often you can sweeten the deal to make a *now* decision seem terribly important. Sometimes a special discount, or free delivery, or special payment terms will spell the difference between a proposition that gets acted on *now,* and one that doesn't get acted on at all.

4. *Where* is the best place for your client to buy the proposition you are selling? Don't just assume your client thinks it's from your firm. Unfortunately, you can spend a lot of time "educating" prospects only to have them go somewhere else when they are ready to buy. I remember calling on a prospect every week to sell him a cash register. Finally, the day came when he was convinced that he needed one. This was on a Friday. So intense did his desire for that machine become over the weekend that he went out and bought one from somebody else (my office was closed on the weekend). What could I have done to forestall this?

5. *How* can your prospect make the purchase you are proposing? It may surprise you that many people fail to act on a desirable proposition simply because they don't know what they have to do, or they don't realize how easy you can make it for them. If you quote a price, say, of $4000 for a computer, and you don't break that down into monthly payments, for example, many people simply will not act, rather than admit they don't have the ready cash. Whatever you do, *don't* assume that everybody regularly uses credit for such purchases. Most people are accustomed to buying such things as automobiles and household appliances this way, but are accustomed to making business purchases on standard commercial terms of something like thirty days net. So if you have *special* terms, don't wait to be asked about them—get them out early.

6. *Why* should anybody want what you're selling? Why should people buy your brand instead of Brand X? Why should they buy it from you instead of from others selling the same product? Sit down right now, and list ten answers to each of these "why" questions. You might also want to do this with each of these six "magic words."

LESSON NO. 39: HOW TO MOVE FROM GREAT GENERALIZATIONS TO POWERFUL PARTICULARS

Particulars Make Sales

Global concepts get agreements, but particulars make sales. You will have no difficulty getting agreement if you continually talk in generalities. However, you won't make many sales. I may well agree with you that motherhood is noble—yet I would not want my teen-age daughter to be so ennobled.

The same situation prevails on a sales call. You could demonstrate a product while talking in terms of how much money the product saves. "Everybody" should want to save money. Right? Well, the fact is that *not every buyer wants to save money in his or her operation right now!* Right now, a buyer may well feel that what's needed is not to *save* money, but to get more from some planned expenditure in another direction. Right now, he or she may well want to *spend* money.

Everybody Talking about Heaven Ain't Going There

This is much like the case of the preacher who asked everybody who wanted to go to heaven to stand up. Everybody stood but one man. His wife nudged him.

"Didn't you hear the preacher? Don't you want to go to heaven?"

"You mean today?" he asked.

This is what frequently happens when we move from generalities to particulars. And this is the reason why you need to be careful in using a presentation that isn't synchronized—that is "out of sync"—with the prospect's *current* needs.

Particulars Are Personal

It happens all the time to salespeople who sell from a large line. A prospect shows intense interest toward one item, but decides against buying it now. "Catch me on your next trip," the prospect says. The salesperson makes a note: "Jack Smith wants the X-14 tool kit for each of his mechanics. Don't forget to bring this up next trip."

"Next trip" rolls around. Jack Smith still likes the X-14 tool kit. But the special price on it, together with the extra sprocket set, doesn't appeal to him (he's not really into saving money this week; this week he's into trying to find ways to increase drive-in traffic. If he doesn't get his volume up fast, he may not be able to make the payroll without going to the bank . . .).

Has Jack Smith lost interest in the X-14? No. Jack Smith *was not interested in the product in the first place.* What he was interested in was the promise of saving money, getting something extra. If the salesperson can somehow tie the X-14 to Jack Smith's *current concerns,* the orginal buying urge will return in greater force.

So What You Say Is True. Who Cares?

Most prospects are too polite to tell you what is truly on their minds. If they did, you might not be able to finish the day, let alone make follow-up calls. Older books on selling placed a great deal of emphasis on getting the client to start saying "yes" as early in the presentation as possible. It has been my experience (as well as the experience of most pros I've talked to), that the value of this kind of "yes" is much exaggerated. The only kind of "yes" you will get at this point is a *global yes; a yes to some generalization; a yes that is virtually meaningless in terms of its sales-producing power!*

At the early stage of the sale in which prospects readily give meaningless assent to meaningless questions, be assured that they also take scant notice of your meaningless generalizations. Hear this word to the wise: pass those "pleasantries" as quickly as possible, and get down to particulars.

LESSON NO. 40: "I'M INTERESTED, BUT I DON'T WANT IT"

Everybody Wants to Be Nice

This is the real reason why it's so easy to get a "global" yes; most people (business people especially) are careful not to hurt the feelings of people they meet during the day—at least if they can "be nice" while remaining noncommittal. Many prospects will even pretend to be interested in your product or service rather than hurt you. But here is a technique that you can use to test the quality of a prospect's interest.

Suppose that you have presented a series of benefits which your prospect seems to be mulling over. Here's the kind of question that will bring forth a meaningful answer:

"These five points are some of the most common reasons that our customers give us for using our services [go over them in skeleton form again]. *Which one of these reasons applies most to your operation?"*

If you get a definite answer to this question, you are in a position to move in with more selling information *around this point of interest.* For example, one salesman sells security services, and one of his strong selling points is that all of his firm's security officers have been thoroughly screened, have passed a polygraph examination, and are bonded. He mentions this fact along with nine other special benefits. When a prospect zeros in on this particular benefit, he pulls out a section of his selling portfolio which has pictures of a number of the company's people, together with a short biography of each officer. He is prepared to talk for several minutes just about this one benefit.

"What Interests You for Later on?"

I have a friend who uses this kind of strategy with a question that ferrets out hidden interests very effectively. She sells cosmetics and uses catalogs and brochures along with personal demonstrations. This pro works quickly and sees a lot of people in a day's time. Her demonstration is brisk, staccato. Many of her customers have already decided on several items as a result of shopping through her catalog, but she's not just an order taker. After writing the order for requested items, she zips through four or five "specials," stopping (just briefly) to ask, "What did you like best of those new items?" Or, "Which of these 'specials' impresses you the most?" When a customer makes a choice in response to this question, she immediately gives a quick selling talk on this one item and tries to add it to the order. However, if she gets a negative response to the question, she asks, "What did you see that you liked, maybe for my *next trip around*?"

Prospects sometimes hesitate to tell you what they like, for fear that this admission will cause you to pressure them into buying. This sales rep allays the customer's fear with the tag " . . .for my next trip around." If the customer makes a choice "for next trip," this saleswoman's next comment is, "OK. Let's see—my next trip will be on . . . ." and she gives a date, following up with, "Will that be soon enough?" Of course, this is a question that is difficult to answer with anything but a "yes"!

Some Customers Are Afraid
to Express Overt Interest

This reluctance to show interest is extreme in some people. I have discovered several reasons for this. Perhaps the most common is the fear of being pressured. But some actually feel it is *impolite* to show real interest unless there is an intention to buy! There is even a cultural predisposition to this attitude that you may find worth watching out for.

Some years ago I was on a cargo ship, going through the Suez Canal. The ship was moving very slowly through the Canal; so slowly that the ship's captain had lowered a ladder over the side to permit "bum boat" merchandisers to come on board and offer their wares to anyone on board who might want them. One person carrying three large baskets of merchandise approached me. He didn't say anything—just smiled broadly and nodded his head as he set his baskets on the deck in front of me. I saw a beautiful pair of suede shoes that I liked.

"Those are nice shoes," I commented. That was about all I got to say. He insisted that I try the shoes on. I did. He told me all about the quality of the leather, the skill used in making these particular shoes. I nodded. Then I took the shoes off and handed them back to him. They were nice-looking shoes, but I had decided I didn't need them. I turned to leave, and the merchant grabbed my arm.

"Wait," he said. "Make your bid."

I didn't want to "bid" on the shoes. I had decided that I didn't even want them. But maybe they were so cheap that I couldn't afford to pass them up. "How much do you want for them," I asked. He told me a price. I shook my head and turned again to leave.

"I really am not interested," I said.

The poor fellow looked at me in utter disbelief.

"You mean you make a man say his price and you're not even *interested*?" he said.

LESSON NO. 41: WHEN CUSTOMERS SAY "NO," BUT THEIR EYES SAY "YES"

The Gambler's Gambit

You've probably heard that some professional gamblers can judge the worth of an opponent's cards by watching the eyes. This may be so. It is also said that ancient jewel merchants could gauge the depth of a person's interest by watching the action of the pupils. This, too, may be true. My experience, however, is that it is very difficult to really watch a person's pupils this closely—at least to do so unobtrusively. However, camera studies of pupillary action made in psychological laboratories prove that pupils do dilate when the subject is intensely interested in some object. Perhaps you will be astute enough to spot these pupillary changes. Some buyers *pretend* such a colossal lack of interest that anything you can pick up this way will be a blessing.

Eye Movements Are a More Reliable Guide

It is difficult to keep looking at something in which you are not interested. The corollary to this is also true: It is also difficult *to keep from looking* at something in which you are intensely interested. Let me tell you about a card trick which will illustrate this principle. Shuffle a deck of cards. Then deal the cards face up, one at a time with a broad movement of the hand so that your subject's eyes will follow your hand motion. Say,

"Think of one of these cards, but don't tell me what it is." Watch the subject's eye movements. His or her eyes will stop following your hand the instant a card is selected! Then after three or four more cards are dealt, the eyes will resume following your hand for a few cards, then will stop again. Try this trick yourself a few times. You will be astonished at how often you successfully "read the mind" of the person watching the trick.

A man who supplements his retirement income by selling uses this principle, selling rings, watches, and costume jewelry to bartenders and waiters two or three evenings a week. He carries an attaché case full of such jewelry, along with a square of black velvet. He lays the velvet on the counter and places several pieces of jewelry on it. As he talks about each piece, he picks it up and sets it off to one side, watching his prospect's eye movements as he does so. If the prospect's eyes remain on one object while he is moving a hand to pick up another object, he knows there is interest, and he concentrates his selling effort on that object.

A salesman who works entirely from a catalog uses this same principle by watching the prospect's eyes as he or she turns the catalog's pages. When he sees the prospect's eyes linger on a page just turned, he turns back to that page and asks questions like, "Just for future reference, do you see anything here that catches your eye? Anything here you'd like to ask me about?"

LESSON NO. 42:
THE SEVEN-POINT INTEREST CHECKLIST

Almost all humans are *already interested* in most of these seven things:

1. *Family*. You can safely *assume* that your prospect is interested in home, spouse, and children. If what you sell can be *instantly* seen to benefit the prospect's family, the result will be *instant interest*. The key concept here is the *instant* recognition of benefit. Thus a padded dashboard, shatterproof glass, and secure door locks need little salesmanship to sell to the mother or father buying a family car. Connections that have to be made symbolically—verbally—like accident insurance don't have nearly the "grabbing" power.

2. *Health*. When you talk about health, it is important to understand whether you mean getting it or keeping it. Many people will risk losing their health for some other gain. Once they have lost it, however, they will spend everything they have earned or can borrow in an attempt to get it back. The product or service that promises to protect health will be interesting to many people. However, if you can find a product which *restores* health, your fortune is made!

3. *Money.* Few things can equal the raw, interest-compelling power of money. Most people would find it absolutely impossible to ignore a one hundred dollar bill lying on the ground—or a one dollar bill, for that matter! And it is *the money itself,* not just the value represented by the money, that works for many people. All of the major auto manufacturers seem to have discovered this at the same time a few years ago when they began giving "rebates" to new auto buyers. Why not just discount the price of the car? Wouldn't that be the same thing? Apparently not—not in the eyes of the thousands of folks who bought cars under the inducement of a $300 or a $1000 rebate!

4. *Security.* Can what you sell protect your client against theft, fire, loss of life? Other loss? Is there some way that you can make your client see the *security* offered by your product or service—NOW? That's the real point of this discussion. Most propositions can be stretched to fit the shape and form of these seven points over time. How *secure* can you make people feel as a result of owning your product? How *quickly* can you show the value of the protection you are offering?

5. *Job or Profession.* You may have read that most people are unhappy with their jobs. That may be true, but the fact remains that few subjects can so dominate a conversation like shop talk. And one of the first questions you will ask a new acquaintance is, "What do you do?" Few things we do are so *identified* with our very beings as are our jobs. For example, a police officer will not say, "I *work* as a police officer." He or she will say, "I *am* a police officer." A firefighter will say "I *am* a firefighter" and never, "I *work* at fires." Want *instant* interest? Show people how to do a job easier, more efficiently. But remember, don't take an hour to get there: Show them NOW.

6. *Social Position.* Can what you sell raise your client's social status? If not that, can it make that status feel more important, or can it in some other way enhance that status? If not the product or service, can *you* do something to raise the client's status—either subjectively or objectively. Perhaps there is nothing you can do objectively, but there is usually something you can do to at least make people feel better about themselves. Look for some way to make your prospect feel that you think his or her job is important. Watch for other social-status signs: awards, trophies, etc. Never fail to comment on any special recognition your client may have received (maybe it was a piece in the paper concerning an advancement. Or an election to office in a service club). When clients see you as somehow contributing to an elevation of their social status, they are interested in you.

7. *Fun.* Are there recreational aspects of your proposition? The vast home computer industry might never have gotten off the ground if it had not been for the fascinating games people can play on their computers. Perhaps you sell something totally devoid of any fun-making potential.

Like anchor chains—or caskets. Be of good cheer. There is no reason for you not to be a fun *person*. You can be the kind of salesperson that clients like to have calling on them. Maybe the old-time "drummer" with his stock of jokes can teach us a lesson or two. Why not make selling a social event? Selling *is* serious business, but it needn't be boring. One thing seems certain: If your client should come to look on your call as a social event, he or she is *interested*.

LESSON NO. 43: THE INTEREST VALUE OF A STRONG DEMONSTRATION

You Can Demonstrate Anything

Even if you sell intangibles, you can put together a demonstration which can take off much of the weight that would be carried by the unsupported word. While you would never want to underestimate the power of a well-organized stock of words, you should be aware that just a handful of exhibits can add real substance to any presentation. It doesn't matter whether you sell tractors or cemetery lots; what you are *really* selling in either case is some intangible concept. Cemetery lots are sold on what's called a preneed basis. And it's certainly not dirt and grass and a headstone behind a chain-link fence that customers are offered. It's freedom from having to make a choice under the pressure of time at the moment of bereavement. And it's opportunity; the opportunity to make that choice coolly, rationally.

How do you say all of this through a demonstration? Well, a demonstration is simply the incorporation of certain tangible "props" into an otherwise intangible presentation. A demonstration enables you to hand things to your clients, enlists their *senses* in your presentation. Your prop might be a machine part or a testimonial letter. It could be a photograph or a graphic display.

Always Do a "Dry Run" First

Remember, everything should work the first time through. Your "dry run" should iron all the bugs out so that the client sees only perfection. No amount of explanation can correct a poor first impression. For a demonstration to run smoothly, everything needs to be organized so well that you never have to look for anything for more than a second or two. Make a list of everything you will use in your demonstration, and check the list against your props just before leaving. If you're going to be making several calls before going back to your office, you will also want to use your checklist between calls to make sure that you are not leaving some important item behind.

**Be Sure to Involve Your Client
in the Demonstration**

Even if it's no more than turning the pages of a catalog, you should get the prospect to participate in the sales process as much as possible. If you are showing some kind of equipment, you should let the client operate it. When showing cost figures, savings, profits, have your client perform some of the math. People *believe* answers they get for themselves.

Spend a Half Hour in a Dime Store

With a bit of imagination and a well-stocked variety store you can find enough props to effectively demonstrate any concept, no matter how intangible it may seem at first. With a bit of practice you can become quite skilled in the use of such things as press-on letters and art. Remember, your "art" needn't look polished or professional—just interesting! And don't overlook the toy department. Many children's games use colorful graphics which you can easily press into service as part of an interesting demonstration.

4

Help Thou
My Unbelief

Perhaps the presentations that you make so captivate your clients that they are intensely interested from beginning to end. If this is true, and they like your proposition, then they will be strongly motivated to believe that you are telling the complete truth. However, no matter how intense their interest and how strong the desire to believe, there may remain a lingering, gnawing doubt. As long as this doubt is there, there will be no true meeting of the minds, and there will be no sale. This chapter shows how to remove those doubts and replace them with conviction.

LESSON NO. 44:
THE VOICE OF CONVICTION

Make Yourself an Expert

You owe it to your clients, to your employer, and *to yourself* to be so thoroughly grounded in the details of your proposition that you can quickly answer almost any question that you are likely to be asked. More than that, however, you need to know the answers to questions that only *another expert* might know to ask. If you are not at that point now, then you will need to set aside at least a couple of hours a day for study and research. In addition to this, you may have to devote almost as much time to attain *verbal mastery* of your proposition. You have probably heard it said that "nothing succeeds like success." This is true. But here's another one for you: *Nothing fails like failure*. It may take you two or three years to build a strong positive reputation as an expert in your field. Fail to do the things you must do, however, and you may find that it doesn't take nearly so long to build a *negative* reputation. Don't be surprised if it only takes two or three months!

Speak with Alacrity, but Don't Be Glib

You must learn to deliver your sales message with considerable swiftness and dispatch. The voice that convinces is the voice that sounds like it *knows*. Try this experiment. Some people delight in giving you the wrong answer when you ask their age. Ask very quickly, "In what year were you born?" How quick is the response? How do you feel about the truth or falsity of the stammering response? The quick response?

There is a tremendous difference between *alacrity* and *glibness*. Even the *sounds* of the words leave different feelings in the nervous system. Speak with alacrity and you speak with promptness, willingness, readiness, eagerness, zeal, enthusiasm, avidity, swiftness, quickness, dispatch, celerity.

Speak glibly and you are smooth-tongued, smooth-talking, fast-talking, oily, unctuous, talkative, loquacious, garrulous, voluble, prolix, verbose, long-winded. Which do you think is the more appealing word?

Studies in the field of social psychology confirm what most people recognize intuitively. The person who speaks with a brisk (but not hurried) pace is far more believable than one who hems and haws or who is continually backtracking. You can only speak briskly, *convincingly* about your proposition when you know the facts thoroughly.

Cultivate a Mellow Tone

Here's another experiment. Put a 33 rpm record on a turntable and play it at 45 rpm. Not only will the singing be *faster,* it will sound higher-pitched. A similar thing happens to the untrained voice when it speaks more rapidly. To get conviction in your voice, keep it brisk, but low-pitched. Keep it mellow.

That's a Good Question—
May I Show You Something on That Later?

Nothing else can slow the pace of a good presentation like a question "whose time has not come." Such questions need to be postponed until they can be answered with more telling effect. In a well-planned presentation, most questions will be answered as the presentation unfolds, and some lose their consequence as a result of a truly *convincing* presentation. An effective way to postpone unwelcomed questions or objections is with a question of your own: "May I show you something on that later?"

Who's in Charge Here?

You absolutely must cultivate the kind of voice that says "I'm in charge" if you expect your voice to carry conviction. You should seek to develop such power in your presentation that you will rarely be interrupted. There are a few tricks of the trade that you can use to assure that you will not be. When you sense an interruption coming just as you are about to make a telling point, hold your hand up, with the palm outward—like a traffic cop's. If you do it with a slight smile (as you continue talking), it will work without offending. Another thing you can do (but it takes practice) is to stop, but keep your mouth open. It may sound funny, but it works.

LESSON NO. 45:
THUMBNAIL TESTIMONIALS

Don't Wait for
Unsolicited Testimonials: Ask

There is an old Chinese proverb which goes, "Man who sits with mouth open waiting for cooked goose to fly in waits a long time." Your product or service may be so good that your customers will be eager to sit and pen (or type) you a letter filled with hearty approbation and lavish praise. But don't count on it. The so-called unsolicited testimonials which advertisers once displayed in their magazine ads are difficult to come by today. Perhaps they were products of a more leisurely era; one even suspects that some may have been figments of an ad copywriter's imagination. Whatever the truth is, they are as rare in our time as the proverbial flying cooked goose. If you're to get an "unsolicited" testimonial today, you're going to have to ask for it!

Brevity Is the Soul of It

The quickest way to get a customer to comply with your request for a testimonial letter is to ask little of him or her. Don't ask for a letter. Confine your request to one for a fifteen-or twenty-word comment; just the briefest mention of his or her satisfaction with *one* feature of your product or service. Example: "The new machine you sold us is the *fastest* we've used . . ." A short note like this is not only easier to get, but a

CEO can even write it out in longhand without waiting for a secretary to type it. And it is more effective than a letter running to two or three hundred words. You can "flash" five or six of these testimonials to a new prospect while you are trying to get them to read one conventional letter.

The company's *letterhead* is what sells them, as much as the content of the letter. In a fast-paced presentation your prospect wouldn't even have to read each letter—you could read them for him. (You will know the contents by heart.) As you run these "thumbnail testimonials" by your prospect, your comments might run something like this: "Jones over at American Foundries says, 'fastest we've ever used . . .'; Johnson at International says, 'cheapest in the long run . . .'; Fred Black at Thermocouple calls it 'the smoothest running on the market today . . .'"

Single Subject Testimonials
Make Cross-Filing Easy

Make a photocopy of your testimonials so that you can file one copy alphabetically, by company name, and another copy according to subject matter. A three-ring binder with clear plastic sheet protectors is ideal for this. Put the alphabetically sorted letters to the front part of the binder and the subject-sorted duplicates near the rear. You'll find that you won't need index tabs for the alphabetical file, since you can easily spot the names on the tops of the letterheads. You may find it handy, however, to have eight or ten subject tabs at the back of the book to help you quickly locate duplicate letters according to subject. These dividers might read something like "Speed," "Economy," "Style," and so on.

Don't Quit with One Letter

A regular customer who is well pleased with your product or service may have several nice things to say about you, your product, and your service. Don't let him or her put it all in the same letter. There may be several features of your product that this customer likes. Why not get a ten- or twenty-word comment on each feature? Most customers will agree to do this if your requests are paced over several visits. On one trip this individual writes you a note concerning, say, "Speed." On another trip, he or she jots down a comment concerning "Economy," and so on. If you are really conscientious about asking for these short notes, you'll find that, in just a few weeks, you will have accumulated an enviable collection of kind words that can make a real difference in your selling.

LESSON NO. 46:
PROVING BENEFITS WITH FEATURES

Features Are Powerful Convincers

Your product's features offer "built in" evidence that your product will really benefit your client in the manner you claim it will. The difference between a "feature" and a "benefit" is one that some beginning salespeople have difficulty grasping at once. An example will make this clear enough so that you will never confuse the two. Suppose that I am trying to sell you a new invention—say a miniature burglar alarm. My device is about the size of a box of matches and is totally self-contained. The fact that it is small and self-contained is not unimportant. But these are *features* which will only be important to clients once they have become *interested in the benefits which burglar alarms confer*. Remember, mere interest in the *features* will not result in a sale, no matter how intense is that interest. An electronics technician who happens to be serving a twenty-year prison sentence might be very interested in this device, and the compact size may really impress him. But he may not be interested in protecting his "cage" against breaking and entry.

Hanging onto the burglar alarm example just a bit longer, let's see how the self-contained, small size helps to prove that my device confers security benefits better, more efficiently. The small size makes it easier to hide so that it can't be disabled by a burglar. If I have discovered that my client takes frequent out-of-town trips, I will show that the device's small size makes it the only burglar alarm that can provide security in strange hotel rooms. But I will never waste time trying to prove these benefits to persons who don't want or need them! That's what you do when you talk *features* before establishing interest in specific benefits.

Breaking into Backtracking

If you sell a complex device with many operational features or sell complex services, you may have to keep reminding yourself not to demonstrate *features*. Again and again you must remember to use these features to prove specific customer *benefits*. This means you will need to check yourself constantly; to ask yourself, "Why am I talking about this feature? What does it prove?" And don't kid yourself into believing that your clients remember those benefits once you have pointed them out. It's up to you to keep reminding them what benefits your features are designed to produce. Keep tying the two together until you have formed a mnemonic bond that can't be forgotten.

Surplus Features
and "Benefits" That Nobody Wants

Once you have mastered the art of strong feature-benefit selling, you'll discover that you rarely have to tell everything you know about your product in order to make a high volume of sales. Most of your clients are buying to resolve some rather narrowly defined area of interest. Several microprocess-based products have the potential for solving an almost infinite variety of problems. It is virtually impossible for the salesperson to touch on more than a small problem-solution set during a demonstration. Computers have been called "do-anything machines." But smart computer salespeople are learning to carve out certain areas of specialization so that sales demonstrations can be kept to manageable proportions. You need to do this no matter what you sell. No matter how many feature-benefit sets you can find, settle on a manageable number of such sets—perhaps a half dozen—and learn to hit hard on them. Your dems will pick up more punch and pizazz as a result.

Customers rarely get hooked on a product which confers no benefit. Salespeople sometimes do! Perhaps it would be more accurate to say that the product confers "benefits" that nobody wants (!?). This is the usual province of the high-pressure sales rep. Such people frequently find themselves having to "create needs," as such selling is euphemistically called, instead of filling needs.

LESSON NO. 47:
HOW TO CONVINCE WITH ENTHUSIASM

The Force of a "Hot Belief"

Power selling is simply not possible for salespeople who have not learned how to create and project the enthusiastic attitude. You cannot long convince others of something which you do not believe in yourself and believe in with *fervor*. You may recall that I said earlier (Lesson No. 17) that *fervor* was one of the five marks of a pro. I also said that most pros have such a "hot belief" in what they are doing that they often experience difficulty "turning it off." It is this one thing more than anything else that *convinces* the client that you are telling the truth; this hot belief makes you come across with sincerity and enthusiasm.

It is possible to build a selling career on nothing but this one quality—that's how important it is. This is the convincing power that all of the world's great ideological leaders have possessed. Learn how to use it, and it will work for you when nothing else will.

Begin by Telling Yourself You Have It

You've heard it many times: Sell yourself on your proposition before you try to sell anybody else. Just how thorough a selling job you need to do may not be clear to you. Let me see if I can say this more forcefully. When you get out of bed in the morning and you stand on the floor, how convinced are you that the floor will be there? Do you have to reach over the edge of the bed and check it out first? Do you have to feel around in the dark with your hands before you will swing your feet out of bed and actually *stand*? Of course not! There is absolutely not the slightest doubt that the floor will be there and will support you when you stand. Now that's how sure you need to be that your proposition will match your verbal description of it. That's how sure you must be that you know the truth about it and will convey that truth to your client.

People come to believe what you tell them over and over again. You are people. You will come to believe what you tell yourself over and over again.

If you sell automobiles, say to yourself over and over until you *know* that it is so: *I am offering the best automobile that can be bought for the money I receive.*

If you sell insurance, say to yourself over and over until you *know* that it is so: *I am offering the finest insurance protection that can be bought for the money I receive.*

Whatever you sell, say over and over to yourself until you *know* that it is so: *I know that this is the best that can be bought for the money I receive.*

You will know that you have developed the fervor you need when you feel this *hot belief* develop as a feeling almost akin to a religious conversion. And when that happens you will know that you have the kind of true enthusiasm for what you are doing that totally convinces others.

Persistence Is Easy
When You Are Enthusiastic

Sheer persistence will convince many people. Having the fortitude to persist comes from being yourself convinced that the proposition you are offering is right for your client. When you have the force of hot belief driving you, you will persist because you are convinced that to give up prematurely would be to do your client and yourself a tremendous disservice.

"I Believe You, but Don't Blink"

Many believe that eye contact is a strong indication of truthfulness. Leaving aside for the moment any consideration of the accuracy of this belief, you should understand that it is the *effect* of this belief that is important at this point. If suddenly people believed that the person with a finger up his nose was a truthful person, then you might want to consider keeping a finger in that position at least part of the time. If your personality is such that you now have no difficulty in making constant eye contact as you talk, then you will not have a problem with this when it comes to selling.

It is probably so that normally truthful persons have more difficulty maintaining eye contact when telling an *unrehearsed lie*. However, with practice it becomes easier and easier to tell a *rehearsed* lie while maintaining eye contact. Admittedly, this is a sorry state of affairs.

The Shifty-Eyed Saint and the Psychopathic Liar

Here is the real connection between the steady gaze and the truthful statement. It is easier to "search for answers" that are inside your head if you are looking away from another pair of eyes. It has nothing to do with truth or falsity, but it does have to do with memory. Of course, it also happens to be true that you need a good memory to be a really good liar.

I have known people who are just about as saintly—and as truthful—as one could be. Yet they cannot look you in the eye while talking to you. On the other hand, I have known people I considered to be psychopathic liars who could look you in the eye without blinking, yet not utter one word of truth.

So what it boils down to is this: If you are an honest person, it will be harder for you to lie while maintaining eye contact than it will be if you are dishonest!

Right between the Eyes

Try this if eye contact makes you uncomfortable. Shift your gaze slightly so that you are looking at a spot *between* the eyes. Your listener will not be able to tell the difference, and it will seem as though you have maintained eye contact all the while. The trick is to keep eye contact as long as you can, but when you need to shift your eyes to avoid discomfort, don't lower your eyes or look away. Instead, shift your eyes only slightly to this between-the-eyes position.

Consider Cultural Differences

No discussion of the fine points of eye contact should ignore certain important cultural considerations. Most books on selling treat the business of eye contact strictly from the viewpoint of the male Caucasian. There is so very much more to the matter. Just a couple of further comments will give a hint of the richness and complexity of the subject. Consider, for example, just a couple of "white-black" differences in eye-contact practices.

White people have a cultural predisposition to look *at* a person while listening, and to look *away* while speaking. Most whites *learn* to look while talking, but this doesn't always come easily. Contrariwise, whites find it easy to maintain eye contact with a person who is speaking. Blacks seem to *prefer* to maintain eye contact while speaking and to prefer to look away while listening!

These observations refer only to American males. American women are another subject altogether. In spite of this, most mention of the subject in books that I have read totally ignores these differences. Scores of interviews with female sales reps have convinced me that women are by far the superior to men when it comes to holding eye contact. This adds yet another reason why women are really coming into their own in at least this one profession—the selling profession.

Before leaving this subject it might help to mention yet another cultural peculiarity. This is the matter of eye contact with persons of various "non-American" cultures. Americans who have traveled to certain Arabic lands, for example, have found that Arabs like to stand very close to each other when they converse and have no difficulty maintaining strong eye contact. Almost all Americans find themselves very uncomfortable in such a situation. Oriental men are also extremely effective in their use of eye contact.

One last word on the subject: Everything I have said about the subject notwithstanding, I believe that the whole business of eye contact has been overdone if you happen to be one of those people who are uncomfortable when attempting to maintain eye contact. With a really effective demonstration, your prospect's eyes will be on the demonstration 90 percent of the time anyhow—so be easy about it.

LESSON NO. 49: ON THE IMPORTANCE OF BEING EARNEST

How to Look Serious without Seeming Silly

Salespeople are constantly exhorted to smile a lot. *It is* important that you learn the art of smiling while you talk; it is important that you "keep a pleasant face." There is an ancient Chinese saying to the effect that an unsmiling man (or, presumably, woman) must not open a shop. It is especially important that you smile during the early stages of the presentation. Now this is not to say that you will be able to *frown* later on. However, there comes a time during every presentation when you will want to create a *heavier tone*. A sales presentation needs to be orchestrated with consummate care. This means that it can't be a matter of guesswork about what mood you intend to create at any particular time.

Do What Other Professionals Do

Your doctor may present a very pleasant face when greeting you at the beginning of an office visit. However, during your next visit pay close attention to how he or she looks when giving you professional advice. You need to cultivate this same serious mien, to develop this "professional look." You will recall the lesson on role playing (Lesson No. 12). If you will prop a mirror up so that you can see yourself when rehearsing, learning the "professional mien" will be a lot easier. By the way, this is another good reason for thorough knowledge of your proposition. It's much easier to come across as a professional when you *are a professional*.

To Blurt Is to Blunder

Although you must know your product so well that you have a wealth of information at your finger tips (or on the tip of your tongue), there will be many times when you will want to avoid blurting out an answer to a problem with which a client has wrestled for days or months. There are several good reasons for this. Not the least of these reasons is the fact that most people like to feel that they are capable of handling most of their problems most of the time, and if they haven't arrived at a solution it isn't likely that you would have such a solution available on a moment's notice! At least pretend to ponder the problem before giving the answer! The thoughtful pause is often much more convincing than the ready reply.

But Seriously, Now . . .

How do you convince the prospect who wants to "play"? Some prospects will adopt a pseudo playful attitude to avoid serious involvement in a proposition in which they are not interested. The only solution to this problem is to somehow *create* interest, or leave. However, once you know you have a strong show of interest, but you can see the prospect slipping away as you bring on your "proof," you will need to guard against such things as this pseudo playfulness. Once you understand that this is simply a defense mechanism—very much like the embarrassed laugh which some people affect—you will know how to handle it.

Try this. Smile warmly. Say something like, "I appreciate a person with a sense of humor. You remind me of another client who (etc., etc.) . . .as a matter of fact, he had a similar problem, and the thing that convinced him was . . ." And here you will slip into an anecdote (Jesus called it a parable) that will illustrate how a particular feature proves a benefit you have claimed for your product or service.

Answering the Frivolous Question

The playful attitude and the frivolous question are two peas from the same pod. Both provide the prospect with a means of avoidance—a way of getting out of a situation which he or she finds uncomfortable. If you have done your job, you will have piled on so much proof that a state of tension is aroused which begs to be released. The prospect either has to buy or rationalize not buying. Playfulness, humor, ridicule, or frivolity can release the tension and furnish the needed rationalization.

When it is obvious that the question is frivolous and not serious, handle with care. Remember that your prospect has changed the dynamics of the situation. The tension has now been released. Laugh lightly. Say something like, "Of course, you're kidding, but you will be interested in knowing that . . ." Now go back into your presentation, and try to build the buying urge again.

LESSON NO. 50: THE CONVINCING POWER OF REPETITION

**The More You Say It,
the More They'll Believe It**

Even a bald-faced lie will be believed if it is repeated many times. Here's how it works. When you hear an unsupported assertion, you will likely believe it if it agrees with something that has already found lodging in your consciousness. It is not even necessary that you have accepted the first bit of information as being true; it is sufficient only that you have not strongly disagreed with it. Now the two bits of information assume a mutually reinforcing character. It is as though you are saying to yourself, "Oh. I've heard that before. Maybe it is true." When you hear it a third time, the feeling becomes even stronger that the statements are true. Now there are *three* bits of information which agree with each other! The fact that all this goes on, on a subliminal level probably makes it even more effective.

Say It Loud, Say It Low—
Say It Fast, Say It Slow

You will say the same thing several times, but that doesn't mean that you'll want to say things *in the same way*. Varying the *form* of your message often disguises the fact that the *content* remains the same. And this is the very thing that keeps the fact of repetition just below the threshold of consciousness where, it is thought, it can more likely register as a *belief*.

There are many ways to add variety to the statements you will propose for your client's acceptance. For example, the first time you give a list of benefits you can put a bit more volume behind your voice than usual. Later, you can repeat this list in a lower tone of voice. Again, you can pick up the *tempo* so that you present your list of benefits at a more rapid pace. Alternately, you could recite the same material at a more leisurely pace.

The Third Time Is the Charm

There seems to be something magic about the number three. Call it superstition if you like, but try it before you pooh-pooh the idea. The famous psychiatrist Carl Jung believed that there was an archetype for this "magical" three in the collective unconscious of mankind. Perhaps there is, as he suggested, a sort of pattern which makes three seem *complete*. Thus there were *three* wise men, *three* blind mice, *three* men in a tub. The list of famous threes is endless. Why *three*? Why not four—or two—or five? I don't know why. But arguments structured so that there are "three reasons," or "three main points," or three of *anything* sound compelling, sound true, sound complete.

You can, I am sure, think of many ways of using this innate urge toward threeness. Here are just three examples:

1. You will like this product for three reasons:
   It is cheaper.

It is easier to use.
There are local service and repair facilities.

2. There are three ways to pay for this:
Open account.
C.O.D.
Cash with order.

3. This is the only major encyclopedia that offers *all three* types of binding: the hard-bound "utility" cover; the luxuriant full-leather binding; the plastic economy cover.

Can you imagine anybody wanting any other kind of binding? Could there be any other kind of binding? Pepper your sales talk with threes like this, and notice how much more convincing your "proofs" sound.

LESSON NO. 51:
THE TOUCHING TRUTH

If I Can Feel It, It's Real

Most of us experience moments of doubt concerning things that we see and hear. If you have ever watched a clever magician, you know that you can be made to believe that you see something illusory; you can be made to see a girl floating in air; later you will see this same girl "sawed in half." Blackstone even made an elephant "disappear" on stage. The eyes can easily be tricked by strategically placed mirrors, dead-black backdrops that secretly hide even large "vanished" objects. A clever ventriloquist can similarly trick the ear to hear a voice coming from a dummy's mouth or from under a chair. But the *sense of touch can rarely be fooled!* We seem to know this instinctively.

When you are puzzled by some phenomenon, you will rarely be content just to get in for a better look—you will almost certainly want to reach out; to pick it up; to touch the thing.

Let Them Feel the Goods

No matter what you are selling, always furnish something for your client to *touch*. You can enlist the sense of touch much more easily for tangibles (from Latin, *tangere,* to touch). But even so-called intangibles almost always have something about them which can appeal to the sense of touch. Sometimes it may take a bit more imagination to find the touching quality of your intangible. But you'll find it if you look hard enough. An investment property, for example, can be given tangibility by building a demo portfolio of 8 × 10 color glossies that the prospect can hold and feel. Ownership in a corporation is symbolized in tangible form with stock certificates, which can be held in the hands. Stock certificates, bonds, paper money, all are given greater *tangibility* by being printed on 100 percent cotton fiber paper, which has a special texture—a feel of *quality* that ordinary wood-pulp paper doesn't have.

Sales presentations that are summarized in the form of a typewritten document, or formal "proposal," acquire added appeal to the sense of touch, in addition to a certain definiteness and permanence that strictly oral presentations lack.

Build a Model

Some propositions, although tangible, have to be sold before the physical property has taken form. New buildings are in this category. Even when there is a physical property, there are times when it is impossible or impracticable to have the prospect hold it or touch it. Even when this is the case, however, it is almost always possible to build some kind of mock-up or model. An acquaintance of mine does a thriving business building such models for architects, shipbuilders, and others.

Feeling Is Owning

The subconscious mind "feels" that touching is owning. Consciously, you know the difference between touching a thing and having legal title to it. Certainly, your client or prospect understands this difference, too. However, there exist within the body-mind system a primitive emotional structure called the *limbic system*. This structure "thinks" that it owns whatever it touches. When this feeling is strong enough, and if there is no *conscious* resistance, there will be a powerful urge to make this possession real. You need only recall the last time you test-drove a brand-new car to confirm this feeling in your own consciousness. The implications of this for the profession of selling are tremendous.

Trying Means Touching; Touching Means Trying

Our "civilized" way of living has caused us to substitute certain symbolic constructs for the touching impulse. We don't ask to *touch* a thing, we ask to "try" it. The fact remains that "trying" *means touching,* and it is the *touching* that causes the limbic system to want to appropriate the object. And it is often the trying/touching that convinces the whole person on conscious and subconscious levels of the *truth* of your proposal.

Memory and the Many Senses of Humans

We are accustomed to thinking in terms of "five senses." Nobody really knows how many senses we have. We try to classify sensory data as visual, auditory, tactile, gustatory, and olfactory, depending on which sense organ such data seem to stimulate. For years it was believed that anything perceived outside of these five senses was the result either of hallucination or of "extrasensory" perception (which simply meant perception *outside* of normal sense channels). Many more senses are now recognized. Perhaps we will one day believe that there are not discrete senses at all, but only a sensing *continuum*. There is, for example, a widespread scientific recognition that we have a sense of balance, a sense of pain, a sense of gravity, a sense of heat and cold.

In order to *convince* people you need to enlist the aid of as many of these senses as you can. But, in addition to this, you should do something that will assure that sensory input is lasting. To help you with this, I will show you an effective way to use what I will call the "mnemonic sense."

Mnemonics; Helping Your Client to Remember

A strong appeal to the senses has a powerful persuasive effect. However, a client may be convinced that your product is as you say it is, yet not be in a position to act on that conviction. Here is an important point that you must never overlook: *Conviction, no matter how produced, cannot last longer than the client's memory of it.* It is absolutely essential that you do something which will assure *retention* of your persuasive efforts.

Suppose you have just demonstrated a new striping machine to the owner of a large shopping center parking lot. Your machine paints straight lines to control parking. The really superior feature of this particular striper is that it has an "electric eye" on the front of it that aligns the machine with a preselected target. Thus you get a precision-painted line in just a fraction of the time required to hand-paint lines. Now you, of course, will want to be as persuasive as you can in your presentation, and you will want to close as soon as you can. But you'll also want to be sure that your prospect *remembers* your proofs if you can't close on the spot. If you have an imaginative manufacturer, you will already be getting help in this area. For example, your machine might be named something like "Cyclops" because of that single central "eye." But maybe not. If it happens to be called the "Z56," you'll just have to rename it! What'll you call it? Why, "Cyclops," of course! Or you might name it the "One-

Eyed Genie." Either name would be evocative; would create a strong image of the special nature of your machine.

It is likely that your prospect may have to convince others and to keep them convinced between calls. Help him or her to do this through the use of mnemonics. Simple devices like this can make the difference between a proof that is remembered and one that is forgotten:

The One-Eyed Genie paints in a straight line—doesn't drip, dribble, or drool.

When you think of the One-Eyed Genie, think of the word FAST: Fast, Accurate, Simple, Thorough.

Suppose that the Genie is a small, compact machine, that it is light in weight, and that it costs less than competitive products:

Remember, there are three important things you'll want to remember about the Genie: it is *littler, lighter, and less.* . . .

Almost any kind of play on words, any alliteration, any acronym or euphony you can introduce here can help your client to remember important benefits and proofs of benefits. Even silly rhyme sounds can help. A woman selling an electronic paging service tells her prospects, "Remember, it's the beeper that's cheaper."

You will probably recognize that this is the technique used by various advertising media. Billboard ads make extensive use of mnemonic techniques, especially the play on words or pun. Pay special attention to those billboard messages that you remember; these same ideas will work for you.

LESSON NO. 53: SOMEBODY MAKES A SALE EVERY TIME

Who Sold Who?

Either you convince the prospect, or the prospect convinces you. Certainly, there are times when your proposition is simply not right for the person to whom you have been trying to sell it. However, if you have done a good job of prospecting and of qualifying your prospects, you should be spending at least 90 percent of your selling time with people who have a need for your proposition and have the means with which to buy it. Assuming that this is so, you should early form the conviction that the people to whom you actually make a presentation *need* what you sell, no matter what they are telling you.

Here is a simple method that will help you to form the *self-*

conviction that you will have to have before you can convince others. During the prospecting/qualifying stage of the sale, try to be as open-minded as you can concerning the matter of prospect needs. A high sense of professional ethics will undoubtedly permit you to accept the possibility that some people do not need your service. Be prepared to accept this condition gracefully.

Build a Force-Field against Prospect Negativity

Once you have accepted that a person does *not* need what you sell, drop that person from your list with peace and equanimity. But the moment you are convinced that a person is, in fact, a true *prospect,* hang on with the tenacity of a junkyard dog. Let absolutely nothing that the person says have the slightest effect on your determination to proceed with your selling program. It is true that you are attempting to establish a consultant-client relationship. This will come about as a result of your convincing the prospect of certain fundamental considerations. But there is also a temporary condition which can only be described as an adversary relationship. You are trying to convince a client that it is to his or her advantage to buy something; the client is trying to convince you that, although he or she is interested in your proposition, there are certain overriding considerations, reasons why he or she should not buy. There is simply no other way to look at it. You are motivated by your need to be of service, but you are also motivated by your need to make a living. The prospect is motivated by a need for what you sell, but *countermotivated* by his or her needs to other things that the money can buy. This is a "macro-micro" dichotomy. A rooster in the barnyard is motivated on a microlevel to do what he does strictly for his own satisfaction. However the hen might feel about it, she is also motivated to run because she is being chased. On the macrolevel, however, these creatures are *not* adversaries, but are partners in the preservation of their species.

The same situation prevails when you attempt to convince a person who is trying to convince you of a contrary proposition. The important point you must keep in mind is that you must remind yourself again and again that you *know* what the "correct" outcome of this mental thrust and parry should be. You *know* that you are both working toward the same goal, no matter what the prospect thinks, and you *know* that the end result will be beneficial to both of you.

You Don't Have to Agree to Be Agreeable

Never agree with a prospect's negative comments, but always be *agreeable.* This is what is meant by the exhortation that you should "agree with your adversary," as the Bible puts it. This means that you should not be *contentious*: it means that you should nod your head up and down before you say "no" to a prospect. For example, it means that if you are asked to do something which you cannot do, and there is no way you can put off giving a negative answer, you would say something like this:

"Miss Brown, I quite agree with you that this item would sell a lot faster at the price you have suggested" (nod head up and down). "But let's see if there is any possible justification for the price I've quoted you." (Continue with your pitch.) Or, if you are trying to be *agreeable* over a complaint about which you *do not agree,* try this:

"Mr. Roberts," (nodding head up and down) "I can see how I would feel that way if I were in your position and had only the information you have right now. Would you take a look at this one point, and see if it helps any?"

You might want to go back and review lesson No. 7 at this point and mull over what we said about protecting yourself against unconscious autosuggestion.

LESSON NO. 54:
PROVING WITH PERSISTENCE

"If You're Back,
You Must Be Telling the Truth"

Often the one thing that identifies a sales rep as a "high-pressure artist" is his or her insistence on a one-call close. Now, I'm certainly in favor of a one-call close when it is at all possible. However, sophisticated buyers today usually realize that there are almost always acceptable alternatives for most products offered in the marketplace. And this means that there is rarely any real urgency to close a deal as quickly as the sales rep would like for it to be closed. There are still plenty of opportunities to push for an immediate decision, but such opportunities more often take the form of added inducements—discounts, free gifts, etc.—for making a quick sale. Always try for a close—you never know when you'll get it. But don't burn your bridges behind you by suggesting (or claiming) that the deal will absolutely not be offered again later.

There is something about that second and third call that adds a special persuasive wallop to your selling efforts. As a crusty old hardware merchant once said to me, "You're still in the neighborhood? If they haven't caught you by now, you must be honest!"

Persistence Is Not Insistence

Aggressive beginning sales reps frequently confuse *persistence* with *insistence*. "Persistence" means "stubborn or enduring continuance." "Insistence" means "continually demanding." People often are convinced by the sheer force of a sales rep's *persistence*. They sometimes *buy* as a result of *insistence,* but they are rarely *convinced* by it! When you are persistent, your deals stick. When someone buys just to get rid of you, don't be surprised if there is a cancellation waiting for you when you get back to your office.

It is sometimes difficult to see yourself as your prospect sees you: Are you perceived as persistent or as insistent? Here is a simple rule of thumb. The persistent sales rep will willingly make several calls rather than antagonize a prospect by pushing too hard. The insistent sales rep usually wants to close now or never! Here's another thing you should watch to avoid being labeled *insistent.* Don't keep trying to prove the same "set" of benefits. For example, if you have been trying to sell a computer based on its capabilities as an accounting system, try concentrating on its word-processing features. That's true *persistence.*

You're a Friend on the Third Call

By persisting through to the third call, you set up an entirely different set of forces. If you have done nothing to antagonize your prospect up until now (good luck!) you are well on the way to establishing a "business friendship." Although we wisely take the advice of such professional "strangers" as doctors and attorneys over the advice of less knowledgeable personal friends, complete strangers are *generally* less convincing than personal friends.

They Need Proof That YOU Believe

Persistence is evidence that *you* believe in what you are selling. It will be very difficult to convince others if you don't have the courage to persist. There is something convincing about the same face time after time, the same hearty handshake, the same warm smile. Nonverbal communication like this can be potent. For this reason, some pros insist on seeing everybody in the territory even if there isn't time to go into a sales presentation. Perhaps as a result of the high cost of making personal calls you will have to forego some of these "show your face" calls; just don't do this lightly.

LESSON NO. 55:
TWICE IS MORE BELIEVABLE

Try the "Buddy System"

Sometimes it takes two salespeople, working in tandem, to convince a difficult prospect. Studies in group dynamics, especially of the difference between *dyads* (two-person groups) and *triads* (three-person groups) have produced insights that should prove useful as you continue to fine-tune your professional selling activities. Consider the situation when two people are involved in any sort of social interaction. If they are to perform a joint action, there is the need for *unanimous* agreement: Both persons must agree (however willingly or unwillingly) to perform the joint action. Lacking this total agreement, there will be no joint action.

Now consider what happens when the group becomes a triad, that is, when a third person is added to the group. Just the simple addition of this one person will change the entire psychosocial nature of the group. The nature and the extent of this change will vary according to the nature of the participants and the type of group (social, business, familial, friendship, etc.), but it will be *nothing like* the dyad group! Decisions now no longer have to be unanimous; if two people in the group agree, the third person will often give in without an argument. Of course, you should understand that we are considering *true groups,* not just collections of people. Three people standing on a street corner waiting for a bus do not comprise a "group" by virtue of the fact that they are all waiting for a bus. It is only when they are *interacting* that group dynamics apply. If the three people were discussing which bus they should all take for a joint sightseeing tour, they would comprise a *group*.

Well, that's enough of the sociology lesson. We have set the stage for looking at what happens when you introduce these concepts into what I've called the "Buddy System." I have seen and used several applications of this system in my selling career, and I have talked to a number of sales pros who almost always use some form of this system on difficult prospects at some stage in the sales process. Quite simply, this is a matter of calling in a third party to back you up when you have exhausted other means of conviction. It's like calling in a witness to attest to your veracity, but it is more than that. Even though your client, in reality, constitutes a "majority of one" when it comes to making the purchasing decision, the fact remains that most prospects are strongly affected by this third-party influence. For example, an insurance salesperson will introduce a third-party "buddy" like this:

"I'd like you to meet Jack Brown. He's especially knowledgeable in the tax angle that I was talking to you about on my last trip . . . "

If you use this approach, it gives you an excuse for bringing in the third party and lets the prospect consider your proposition from a fresh perspective. The same thing will happen when you reciprocate as the "expert" when calling on one of your buddy's clients.

Take Your Boss Along

Your sales manager may add that extra authoritative push that is needed to tip the scales in your favor. Long-time pros sometimes get into the lone-wolf consciousness, and that's too bad. Of course, it might not be the sales manager's fault. If a top pro outproduces everybody on the sales force, why not leave well enough alone? One of Murphy's Laws is that if you fix a thing that's not broken, you'll break it. If you're one of *your* company's top people, you may not even remember who your sales manager is! Maybe you are convinced that you don't *need* your sales manager with you. Try it once in awhile anyhow. That "extra" sale might pay for a super evening out for you and a special friend.

Two's Company

You need to keep a full head of steam, to stay "up," in order to be truly convincing. Selling can be a lonely business, and having a friend with you, perhaps once or twice a month even, can be a big boost to your morale. Of course, the smart rep will take full advantage of the power of this emotional "fix." I know a branch manager for a chemical firm who works with his top people in what he calls a "round-the-clock sellathon." The program is completely voluntary, but he has no trouble finding a salesperson to work with him *nonstop* for twenty-four hours, one day each month! He claims that there are enough industrial plants running all night long where a departmental buyer (usually a foreman—or forelady) will see him. He says this would never work if he asked a sales rep to do it on his or her own. I have no doubt he is right.

LESSON NO. 56: "IT MUST BE TRUE: I SAW IT IN PRINT"

The Convincing Power of the Printed Word

Written proposals add conviction to your sales talk. If you don't know how to use a typewriter, now's the time for you to learn. You needn't type eighty words a minute to knock out attractive and impressive written proposals which can add tremendous persuasive power to your presentation. Just two or three pages of neatly typed material can make a real difference. If you've been toying with the idea of buying a personal computer, this might be the excuse you need. You needn't really learn anything but "hunt and peck" if you wish—especially if you use a computer keyboard instead of a typewriter. You will make corrections on the screen before printing anything out. An attractive alternative to a computer (and quite a bit cheaper) is one of the new electronic typewriters that have lift-off correction capability. However you do it, I urge you to add this dimension to your selling right away. I have sold many things by combining an oral presentation with a typewritten proposal. As a writer, I have sold thousands of dollars worth of writing services this way. In many instances I have sold such literary properties using nothing more than a written proposal, outlining my ideas for the completed piece of work. And that includes my ideas for the book you are reading now. No matter what you sell, it started out as an idea, and that idea can be given tangibility and permanence, apart from the object, on paper.

Write Your Own Guarantee

You may want to check with your sales manager to see how far you can go with this, but consider the possibility of writing a proposal which puts in written form the promises you have been making about your product's performance (you really do mean what you've been saying, don't you?). One sales rep added even more strength to this idea by adding a special twist of his own. When he was ready to close, he said something like this:

"Mr. White, I have written down all of these claims for you. Now I'm going to sign them. You will see that I am putting everything in this envelope, which is addressed to you. I have affixed a stamp to this envelope. When you get a chance, drop this envelope in any U.S. Government mailbox. When you get this back, through the U.S. mail, you will know that if I have lied to you about any of the particulars of this proposition which I have put in writing, then I have done something which could easily land me in prison. I will have used the U.S. mail to defraud you. I believe you know that I am not about to do that!"

The Notarized Statement

For some people, an affidavit is gospel. There is something about an embossed seal on a sheet of bond paper that almost defies them to doubt the veracity of the statement to which it attests. Several mail-order promoters of books and of business "plans" have made extensive use of "sworn and notarized" statements. There are any number of ways that this idea has been used; your imagination will undoubtedly suggest yet more ways.

A used car dealer shows a notarized document which is clipped to the title of each car on his lot. The document contains the sworn statement of a well-known independent auto mechanic who has examined the car and who attests its serviceability.

A typewriter shop provides similar documentation, only it is the firm's own service people who sign an affidavit before a notary (the firm's secretary), attesting that they have performed a ten-point service and/or repair operation.

LESSON NO. 57:
PROVING YOUR POINT WITH QUOTES

"If Somebody Else Said It, It Must Be True"

A *direct quote* is a convincer that is hard to beat. No matter what the product or service is, nobody really wants to be a pioneer buyer. We want to be thought of as modern; progressive, but not brash or foolhardy. This is one reason why a good stock of quotes from satisfied users is invaluable. An equally important reason is that a series of quotes acts like a parade of witnesses in a court trial.

In this lesson, I am making a distinction between what I call a "quote" and what I call elsewhere a "testimonial." I reserve the term "quote" for a brief *memorized* statement, repeating what one of your clients has told you. It is important that you memorize these statements and the names that go with them. It is true that you could simply use your own words in telling about a particular benefit, but people tend to give greater credibility to what we say when we can show that *others* believe as we do.

How to Package Your Collection of Quotes

Get business cards from all of your *happy* customers. On the back of each card make a three- or four-word note (a future quote) concerning what this *happy* client has told you. You may have noticed that I am making another distinction here—between *satisfied* clients and *happy* clients. A satisfied client is one who has no complaint about your product or service and will probably be willing to give you a *written* testimonial if you ask for it. A happy client is one who is *enthusiastic* about your product and will almost try to sell anyone who calls to ask about it. Get testimonials from satisfied clients—get quotes from happy clients.

Make photocopies of a bunch of business cards at the same time, and cut the sheet up so you have individual copies. When you quote these people, say something like this:

"Bill Jones told me he's *never* had trouble with his machine, and he bought it five years ago." Now, hand this prospect one of the card copies and say: "Here, he'll be glad to confirm this. Give him a call." If you combine these quotes with a couple of pertinent written testimonials over a period of time, even the most doubting prospect will likely come around.

The "Live" Quote Technique

Somewhere among your happy customers there are at least a couple of men or women who are so pleased with your product or service that they can't wait to tell somebody else about it. These are people who won't mind being called on the phone at almost any time and asked for an opinion of your product. If you have customers like this, save them for use on really difficult prospects. You won't want to "burn out" your good quotes by using them too often. Here's how this works. When you reach the crucial point—perhaps right after showing a couple of testimonials or quotes—say something like, "But listen—I know a guy [or gal] who had a problem similar to yours and who has really become a good friend since learning how to solve this kind of problem using my product. May I use your phone?" Then, call this happy customer up. Hand the phone to your prospect, and say something like, "Ask how she likes it. Ask whether it solved this problem as I've claimed it will."

Here's an important tip on the use of "live" quotes in this manner. Never use them unless you are at a spot where you can logically believe that your prospect is ready to make a closing decision. Then, right after the prospect has received a reply over the phone and hung up, cock your head slightly to one side and wait for a comment from your prospect. *Don't say a word until the prospect does, no matter how long you have to wait!* It is quite reasonable for your prospect to say at this point, "Okay, I'll take it." Act as if you expect that this is exactly what is going to happen.

The Electronic Quote

Here's another use for the tape recorder. This is almost as good as the live quote (except for the closing gambit just mentioned). And with it y ou can really liven up a sales demo. Try calling a few of your *happy* customers, and ask them to make a comment or two "for the record." Use a hookup like that described in *Lesson No. 13* to record your conversation. However, in this case you will want to do something a bit different prior to reaching your client on the phone. While the phone is ringing, speak into the phone (and consequently into the recorder), saying something like, "I'm calling Jack Smith about the comment he made to me concerning the Z25." This will help to identify the proper segment of the tape, as well as identify the subject of your call for later prospects. Playbacks of these quotes can be most impressive to potential clients.

5

The Emotional ''Bump'':
Key to Prospect Eagerness

I've chosen to call the subject of this chapter a "bump" rather than a push, a shove, or a nudge for two reasons. First, I think that it is important for you to realize that it can happen to the prospect as a result of something *outside* of the sales process as well as from something you do during the presentation. The second reason is that it is vital that you appreciate the necessarily *gentle nature* of this influence. As one lesson in this chapter points out, should your prospects feel that you are *manipulating* them—playing on their emotions—you might just as well pack up and leave.

LESSON NO. 58:
THE POWER OF EMOTION

Selling Is an Emotional Experience

Selling is an emotional experience, and so is buying. If you intend to do more than take orders from people who are ready to buy, you must learn to touch a prospect's emotional "hot button." How do you know what "button" to press? Is your prospect quality-oriented or economy-oriented? Do you push the "profit button" or the "prestige button"?

When in Doubt, Press Them All

If you were to get on a self-service elevator and the door closed, but the elevator would not move when you pressed the button for your floor, what would you do? You'd probably press some other button; maybe you'd press them all, trying to find one that would cause the elevator to move. You'd likely do something like this if you turned your car radio on and your favorite radio station didn't respond when you pressed the proper button.

Knowing a Customer Means Understanding

The more calls you make on a particular customer, the better you will understand this business of emotional drive, and the more certain you will be of which "button" to press. However, in the beginning and when calling cold, it will help if you are careful to structure your presentations so that they include benefits which satisfy *several* emotional needs.

Psychologists have listed scores of emotional needs, and "need theory" has been in and out of favor during the past few decades. However, the following list—while not all-inclusive—has proven useful in understanding the emotional factors which influence the selling/buying process:

Achievement. This might best be described as the need to do something difficult. The person with "high Ach" will have a strong drive to manipulate, organize, and assert mastery over objects, people, and ideas.

Affiliation. This is the need of a "joiner," someone who likes to cooperate and to engage in reciprocal activities with others perceived as kindred souls.

Aggression. One who is feeling this need will feel impelled to overcome opposition by force—physical force or verbal force. At the very least, he or she will like a good argument.

Autonomy. The need for autonomy is the need to remove oneself from domination by others; it is the need to feel free and independent and to be able to act on impulse when the opportunity presents itself.

Dominance. This is the need to influence or direct the behavior and activities of others. Persons strong in this emotional need will seek to assert this dominance either by persuasion or command; by suggestion or seduction.

Exhibition. The exhibitionist needs to make an impression and to be seen or heard—or both.

Nurturance. This is the strong desire to take care of those perceived to be helpless.

Order. Neatness is important to one feeling this need. So are cleanliness, order, arrangement, balance, precision, tidiness.

Play. This is the desire to act for the fun of it, without further purpose.

Sentience. The need for sensual experiences.

Safety. The need to feel safe from harm.

Affection. The need for friendship and love.

Esteem. This is the need for a strong self-image, and the need to feel that others hold one in high regard.

Needs Are Not "Types"

It is really not correct to say that one customer is a "nurturing type," while another is, say, an "affiliational type," as though they were mutually exclusive. The truth is that we all exhibit most of these needs at different times. However, a particular product or service can satisfy certain of these needs for some people. It may satisfy quite different needs for others. Your job is to determine which will do which, and when.

LESSON NO. 59: SELLING AND THE RIGHT HALF OF THE BRAIN

Selling Is More Than Talking

The prototype of the fast-talking salesman has been with us for a long time. This image is so deeply imbedded in our consciousness that it has become a most difficult one to rid ourselves of. That's a shame, for it's long past time that the true professional in the field of salesmanship became aware of the changes that have taken place in the area of interpersonal communications. Buyers today have reached a level of sophistication which enables them to more easily penetrate the "fog" exuded by fast-talking flimflam artists. Today's buyers rely far more on nonverbal messages.

Actions Are "Louder"

Recent behavioral studies suggest that, for most people, the *left* hemisphere of the brain processes information through the use of verbal symbols. The *right* side of the brain, on the other hand, is more spatially oriented. This side of the brain is acutely aware of thousands of things that are happening in the environment; things that are mostly not verbalized at all. Such technological advances as television have made us more aware of nonverbal symbols, less trustful of verbalisms. Because of television, there is now greater opportunity to *see for ourselves,* rather than going by what somebody *tells* us. This right-brain processing makes a buyer more interested in what a salesperson *does,* as opposed to what he or she *says.* Actions really are louder than words when it comes to selling today.

Convincing the Right Half of the Brain

When was the last time you went downtown to hear a famous "orator" speak? Listening to such public speakers was once a popular form of entertainment. Wars have been waged, religious crusades launched—all because someone had the power to whip a populace into a frenzy by the power of unsupported speech.

Many salespeople operate as though words still held such mighty sway. You've got to *show* today's buyer. You do this with powerful visuals and forceful graphics. You do it with demonstrations that permit people to touch—sometimes even to taste and to smell. You do it when you add action to your presentation.

Facial Gestures and the Right Brain

Motion pictures and television have sharpened our awareness of the importance of facial expressions. Through these media we have been able to study the facial gestures of others without embarrassment. Actors today learn to express feeling more by facial gestures than by voice. But what does this have to do with selling? Is a salesperson an actor? You bet! And if you think that it is more "honest" to always express your "true" feelings, consider this. *The activity of acting can of itself engender feelings which you at first "pretend" to have!* If you have a strong desire to like a person (perhaps because you realize that it is important that you do), begin at once to *act as though you like that person.* In a very short order you will not be acting at all, and the right-brain processing of the other person will recognize this *new truth* as it is expressed in your facial gestures. This accords with the psychological theory of *cognitive dissonance,* which says that our actions and our feelings tend toward *consonance* (agreement, harmony). According to the theory, if we find ourselves acting contrary to our feelings, we will usually do something to cause either the feeling or the action to change so as to come into agreement with the other. Professional salespeople who have checked this out have found themselves in agreement with the countless psychological experiments conducted by researchers.

Mirror, Mirror, on the Wall

Spend fifteen minutes a day in front of a mirror. Be sure that your face is sending the same message as your voice. Watch your eyes. Do they smile when your mouth does? The eyes are capable of a much wider range of expression than most people realize. There is the wide-eyed expression of surprise and of rage, the narrow eyes of an icy contempt, the "Santa Claus" eyes of happiness and mirth. Some actors have learned a trick with the eyes, in which the muscles below the lower lids move up while the upper part remains stationary; this conveys the feeling of pleasure and affection. One other word on facial gestures. Get in the habit of *smiling while you talk,* and avoid the theatrical, broad expanse of ivories that nobody really believes.

LESSON NO. 60:
THE PERSONAL-QUESTION TRAP
IN CROSS-GENDER SELLING

How to Field Personal Questions

Whether you are a woman calling on a male prospect or a man calling on a woman, it can happen to you. The prospect can ask you a question about your personal life. The question may seem innocent enough. But the professional approach to using emotional power in selling requires a high order of diligence and understanding. Even the seemingly innocent question, if it is not handled properly, can have a devastating effect on an otherwise flawless presentation.

There's a trick to handling these questions. First, understand that there is sometimes an attempt by the other party to establish a personal relationship. *Understand* what the question means, but *don't acknowledge that it means that.* The trick is to make the other party feel that you are there only on business, but to do this in a way that won't bruise an oversensitive ego.

The Two Most Common Questions

Spotting an exposed ego in time to avoid tripping over it becomes easier when you learn to avoid early the trap of the personal question, says one sales rep. She has found that there are two questions which are almost always intended to pave the way for some sort of personal relationship. The first question is "How long have you been in town?" The second is "Do you have children?" She has found that this first question is an invitation for her to talk about herself rather than about her business proposition. The second question attempts to learn, in a somewhat circuitous manner, whether she is married or not, and the questioner usually intends to follow with a personal disclosure of his own.

Refocus the Prospect's Attention

Regardless of the intent of the personal question, the professional sales rep doesn't take offense—nor give it. And this is avoided by quickly rechanneling or refocusing the interest of the questioner. A quick and efficient way of doing this—and one that offends no one—is through use of a transitional expression. A transition is a rhetorical device which moves a listener smoothly from one thought to another, usually dissimilar thought. If the transition is made skillfully, the listener will often not even be aware of the trip he has been taken on.

Newscasters use this strategem in moving from one news story to another, and some are so good at it that you can watch a well-done telecast almost without realizing that you are watching several totally unconnected stories. Once you start using these transitions, you will find many applications for them. For the time, however, we'll confine our study to using transitions in cross-gender sales situations.

For example, the salesperson could answer the first question with something like, "I've been here two years. And before that I lived in Chicago, where I sold stocks and bonds. This gave me the kind of experience I needed to feel confident in advising you about the sort of investment we're considering now. . . ." The transitional device will work with almost any kind of personal question. The question about children, for instance, might be handled like this: "I have two children, and I have been able to provide for their college education through the use of just the kind of investment that I am recommending to you. Now here's how this would work. . . ."

What Kind of "Vibes" Do You Give Out?

A top investment counselor says that when she first started in the business she discovered that she was giving out PLOM ("Po' li'l ol' me") vibes to some of her male prospects. In the beginning, sales were small and far apart. She says she soon learned that she needed to make several corrections in the way she presented herself. First, she decided that she needed to dress in a more professional manner—a manner which better matched the attire of her male prospects and clients. This didn't mean, however, dressing in a more severe or "mannish" fashion. Second, she eliminated all personal references to herself and concentrated on making her *presentation* so totally captivating that personal questions would be less to likely arise.

LESSON NO. 61: SELL YOUR SONG—DON'T GIVE IT AWAY

Put Feeling into Your Presentation

It takes more than a beautiful voice to sing at the Met. Most of what you read about harnessing emotional power suggests that it is the *prospect's* emotions that are involved. Of course this is true, as far as it goes. However, as mentioned before, buying *and selling* are emotional experiences. It is unquestionably true that you will never perform like a star until you learn to push the right "hot buttons" to activate your client's emotional drive for possession. But you will also need to activate, to manage and control, *your own emotional power* as well! This is what it takes to make a *star* in sports, acting, singing, and selling.

A beautiful voice alone will never propel a singer into stardom. "Sell your song—don't give it away" is the way show-biz savants put it. Put feeling behind everything you do. When you wrap your proposition with your own emotional power, you sound more *real*. You sound as though *you are convinced* of the value of your proposition. And this is far more important in the mind of your client. Far better is it to him that you sound *convinced* than that you sound *convincing*!

They Buy Your Act First

The analogy seems appropriate. A top producer is almost always a fantastic actor—even an entertainer. He or she is usually one who has learned how to create and maintain a special personality which customers "buy" before they buy the product. Consider how some of the all-time entertainment greats did this. Louis Armstrong was a trumpet player of considerable merit. His *singing,* on the other hand, was nondescript, to put it kindly. But what he lacked in singing ability he certainly made up for with that special emotional quality called *charisma*. Anyone who has ever heard him "sing" will never forget the sound of his voice—a delightful rasping, gravelly sound like one might produce by dragging a file across a rusted tin can. Louis "Satchmo" Armstrong understood that *you don't give your song away—you sell it*. And he understood that *you must get people to buy your act before trying to sell your song*. They have to buy your personality before they can accept what you are selling.

Beginning salespeople frequently ask, "How can I pretend to feel something I don't?" They miss the point. You don't *pretend* to feel something. It's the same with *creating* an exuberant, enthusiastic sales personality. *You don't pretend to be some person that you are not*. To begin with, you must realize that a personality is not what you are. What you *are* is a lot more complex than that, and I'll forego that argument. What I'm talking about is the *persona,* the mask all of us wear, the role(s) we play. It is because we are role-playing creatures that we are able to handle such diverse functions as, say, that of an aggressive prize fighter and that of a tender, loving father at the same time. This is possible only because of a thing called *role-specificity.* Both roles are handled at the "same" time when they are considered in relation to a larger time frame, such as a lifetime. The roles are played out, however in much smaller time frames. The tender, loving father doesn't have to be aggressive. Neither does the prize fighter need to act kind and loving toward his opponent.

Take a moment and list all of the "roles" you are required to play in a day's time. Now consider how many different roles you might play in a year. Most of these roles require at least slightly different "personalities." Some require radically different personalities. In most cases, each role-specific personality was created by the demands of the role: There was already a model of how a mother should behave before you became a mother, a model of what a father should be before you became a father. If you are president of a club, the president's role (and the president's "personality") was there long before you arrived. But you can just as easily *create a personality* as slip into one that has been created for you by the demands of a role. And that's what you do when you create a special sales personality.

First, Get a Model

To create a sales personality, you will first need a model. You may take as your model a living person who is acting now or who has acted in the desired manner. Or you may even create the model! Your own imagination combined with the suggestions in this and other books on selling will help you. Write out a detailed description or "blueprint" for the personality you wish to build. Be careful not to make this a godlike personality that would take several lifetimes to build. Be optimistic, but be realistic. Here is a tip that can save you a lot of grief: First write a one-page description of the way you see yourself (or rather your *personality*) at the present time. Then pick one area of your personality you wish to change in the direction of the new personality you are trying to create. For example, you may perceive your present personality as being too contentious, too argumentative. You could realistically expect to improve this one personality aspect. So rewrite the description of your present personality, but in this new description *include the desired change.* Work on this one thing for at least a month before adding another quality from your "ideal" personality profile. If you keep this up for a year, you will see an astounding difference in the way you come across to your clients and prospective clients.

Leave Them Wanting More

Here's one more piece of business you should remember as you learn to add more charisma to your selling personality. It too is borrowed from the sister-profession of acting. It is a maxim that the real stars of show business *never* forget. Second-raters caught by the pull of their own egos often violate this rule. How you handle it will in large measure determine where *you* will rank. Here's the rule: *Always quit before they've had enough.* It's a tough rule to follow, for the borderline may be an extremely fine one. The trick is to push very close to the limit without going over.

LESSON NO. 62: THE "DESIRE" STEP: WHAT DOES IT REALLY MEAN?

The One Vital Component

If the customer's desire to possess your product is strong enough, you can leave out all of the other "steps" and you will still have a sale. If the desire to own is *not* present, there will be no sale—even if you are the world's strongest closer. Fortunately for most salespeople, many prospects come to the sales presentation with some desire for the product already built by advertising or by exposure to the product through friends or family.

Strong Desire Compels

Other factors *impel*: strong desire *compels*. You can arouse strong desire for ownership only by constantly drumming on those benefits of your proposition that promise to satisfy one or more of the prospect's emotional needs (see Lesson No. 58). Once you find out what motivates your prospect, keep talking about how your proposition can satisfy the need. Think of at least five different ways you can express this need and at least five different ways in which your proposition can satisfy it.

Futile Logic and Strong Desire

In the face of a powerful emotional pull, an intense desire outweighs all the "logic" you could use. Here's an example. Suppose you are selling a small computer system. You know that your prospect only needs a system with the software to handle his accounting and billing chores. You know that he doesn't write five business letters a month, so you don't even mention expensive word-processing packages. However, unbeknown to you, a competitor has learned that your prospect is a frustrated author who has papered his walls with rejection slips for the stories he has written in his spare time. The competitor correctly surmises that this thwarted authorship operates as a powerful emotional motivator. Your competitor sells the same system you sell for the bookkeeping and billing, but goes a step farther: He "throws in" the word-processing package at "his cost." It's easy to see, isn't it, that your logic could be flawless and still fail to convince in the face of the emotional satisfaction that your prospect has envisioned.

Outside Sources of Desire

Some desires that motivate your clients or prospective clients will be aroused by you. Every real pro has a collection of emotional motivators and is ready to supply them as the need arises. But, as was the case just mentioned, there will sometimes be a powerful motivator—a strong desire for a *competing* product or service is *already at work*. At times the prospect will tell you about this. Most of the time, however, you will have to ferret this information out for yourself. And it is at this point that you could blow the whole thing. If the prospect should do you the favor of telling you about his or her interest in another product, the temptation is great to institute a selling blitz designed to show the superiority of *your* product. The professional thing to do is just the opposite of this. *Try to get the prospect to sell you on the competing product!* Again, if you're lucky, you will learn all about your competitor's product from your prospect's point of view. From the utilization planned for this product, you will get valuable insight into what motivators your competitor has appealed to in attempting to sell his or her product, and you will learn which of these motivators actually touched your prospect. In short, you will learn which "hot buttons" your competitor has discovered. You'll learn more about the prospect's emotional needs than you could in an hour of probing.

Satisfy, But Don't Pander To

Everyone has emotional needs, but nobody likes to be reminded of them. Few people would admit that they made an important purchase simply to satisfy an emotional need. Thus, one who buys a luxury car prefers to talk about "investing," not about buying. To continue with the analogy, suppose you are selling such a car. To begin with, *you* wouldn't call it a "luxury car." This is true even if your prospect *exudes* opulence. You'd demonstrate your product in such a fashion that nobody could overlook the car's luxury qualities—but you'd call these qualities something else. For example, in pointing out the deep rich velvet seat covers (even if they are royal purple and you're selling to a prince), you might say something like: "The women and girls will like the warmth of these seats so much better than plastic. And the fabric is treated to guard against stains, to protect your investment."

**Prestige: Many Want It,
Few Will Admit They Do**

There is no way you can sell prestige with a frontal approach. Most people would not even admit to wanting it. Talk to a man or a woman who is being given a promotion that carries additional prestige. Unless the new job requires a truly onerous increase in work or responsibility, many people will accept such a "promotion" in lieu of a raise in pay! Most, however, will tell you that they did so for a variety of *other* reasons, and will not even mention the word *prestige*. Instead, they will tell you things like "the job gives greater exposure to the corporate structure." Or "the new position affords increased visibility." Which is another way of saying, "The boss and I get to see each other more often, and everybody else sees us, too." The smart employer, like the smart sales rep, learns not to let people feel that their emotions are being played on.

Don't Use a Trowel

Flattery goes on with a trowel, genuine admiration with a sable brush. Genuine praise is much more difficult than flattery. To begin with, you won't really have anything to praise a stranger about. You won't know enough about such a person to give meaningful praise, for one thing. There is a positive danger that what you intend as praise will be taken as flattery. Dale Carnegie was undoubtedly right when he counseled "hearty approbation and lavish praise," but in attempting to use praise as a lever to motivate a client, you will want to proceed with extreme caution. One office supply sales rep says that she avoids this pitfall by confining her praise to *objects,* until such time as she knows the prospect very well.

"I just pick out something in the office that is really unusual—something I can honestly admire. If my prospect is responsible for acquiring it, he or she will *feel* praised. If somebody else deserves the credit, no harm will be done. On the other hand, if the object has special significance, it could lead to something more meaningful. I saw a beautifully inlaid miniature chest on a client's desk and asked excitedly where he'd gotten it. It turned out that his daughter had given it to him. This led to his showing me pictures of his daughter, who was away at school, and to other personal disclosures. She was a beautiful girl, and I told him so. He accepted this indirect praise from me with ease and grace, because it didn't require that he pretend any false modesty."

Say It with Quotes

This an almost sure-fire method of praising a prospect without causing embarrassment. Couch the praise in terms of a direct quote from somebody else. For example, "John Stout over at Fidelity says you're one of the most knowledgeable shop foremen in the business." Be careful in using this kind of quote that it is completely truthful. A salesman calling on large auto-repair shops uses this type of quote and accumulates such quotes along with the quotes and testimonials discussed earlier. He says that using a "blind quote" works almost as well. This is where he says something like, "A couple of my clients have told me that you've been running shops for thirty years and that if I wanted to know anything about cars, I should ask you." He says he always gets a laugh by following up with this question: "Do you agree with their high opinion of you?"

There is one phrase in this quote that gives it the ring of truth even though the quote has no name attached to it. You have probably spotted it: It is, of course, the phrase "running shops for thirty years." The prospect, on hearing this could be expected to think something like, "This guy must be telling the truth. How else would he know that I've been running shops for thirty years?"

LESSON NO. 64: THE "JAM PITCH": EMOTIONAL BONFIRE

The Strongest "Joint" on the Midway

Here is a sales "pitch" that is extremely powerful in its emotional appeal. In its heyday, this kind of selling was frequently seen on carnival midways. The power of the *jam pitch* was such that operators of other concessions would often refuse to sign with a carnival that allowed a *jam pitch* to operate.

The science of astronomy developed from astrology, and chemistry evolved from alchemy. To study such modern scientific disciplines as astronomy and chemistry, we needn't learn the details of their antecedents. This is surely also true of the study of modern professional selling. But a dip into our not-too-glorious past (when salespeople were called pitchmen, hucksters, peddlers, or drummers) may prove illuminating.

Here's how the jam pitch worked. Pay special attention to the emotional elements. The jam pitchman usually worked from a platform set up at the rear of a large tent with side walls that could be rolled up and dropped as needed to control the crowd (or "tip," as it was called). Shelves to the rear of the platform were loaded with such merchandise as radios, toasters, watches, electric razors, writing pens, and a wide assortment of other items. As the crowd of people coming onto the carnival midway walked in front of his tent, the pitchman began passing out "free samples," like packages of razor blades, small sample tubes of shaving cream, hand cream, styptic pencils.

The Sucker's Dream: Something for Nothing

"Here it is, folks. The only free attraction on the midway. Not only that, we pay you to attend," the jam-pitchman said. He quickly passed out several samples. As soon as he had stopped enough people to block the flow of traffic down the midway, he said something like, "I'm sorry, folks—we're blocking the midway. Kindly step forward. . . ." He began to back into his tent. Two or three assistants (called *shills* or *sticks*) who have been mixing with the crowd begin to push forward so that those in front of them move toward the tent. Soon a group of twenty or so are inside the tent. The pitchman moves to the rear, passing out "free merchandise" (as he calls it now). He steps up on the platform and picks up a "sample" that is a bit more valuable than what he has given out before. "OK, who wants a free pack of cigarettes?" Twenty hands go up. More people press in. "Hold it. *Hold it*! I've never seen so many dirty hands in my life!'' The crowd laughs. ''Put 'em down. The manufacturer has only furnished ten packs for me to give away at each show.'' (This is a blatant lie. The ''manufacturer'' had only ''furnished'' the cigarettes via the corner grocer, where the pitchman had bought them.) ''Okay. Tell you what—the first ten people who raise their hands . . .'' Fifty hands go up (the ''tip'' is getting larger as newcomers crowd in to see what the excitement is all about). ''Come *on,* folks.'' Good-natured laughter from the tip now. ''Put your hands down. Let's see, now. . . .'' The pitchman pretends to ponder how he's going to distribute the ten ''free'' packs of cigarettes. ''I'm going to put a nominal charge on this one to make sure that only those who really want them get them. Who'll give me a nickel for a pack?'' Just as many hands go up as before. He singles out one person. ''You, sir. I think you were one of the first. Will you give me a nickel?'' The man gives him a nickel.

''Thank you for the nickel,'' says the pitchman. ''Tell me, is that a good deal?'' The customer agrees that it is. ''Then, since you've been such a good sport, I'm going to give you another nickel. Is that a fair return on your investment, or is it not? Now, who'll give me a dime for this next pack?'' The pitchman points to somebody with a hand up. ''You, sir, give me a dime.'' The trade is made. ''Enjoy your cigarettes. Have you made a fair trade? Good! Here's your dime back—and another dime profit.'' The pitchman quickly runs through several packs of cigarettes, increasing the ante for each pack until he is up to a dollar. He follows the same procedure as before, giving the dollar back and adding an extra dollar. By now the collective emotion of the tip has increased tremendously.

The Emotional Appeal to Greed

The pitchman correctly surmises that there are a goodly number of people in the *tip* who are emotionally ready to gamble on his veracity, if not his honor. He picks up a silver-plated cigarette lighter.

''I have five cigarette lighters to pass out. Let me see five people who want them.'' Perhaps sixty or seventy hands go up. ''Never mind. Let me see five people who'll pay a dollar for one of these lighters. You, sir. Hand me your dollar. Here's your lighter. Satisfied with your purchase? Good! Here's your dollar back, plus a dollar for participating in this advertising program. Who'll give me two dollars for this next lighter? Thank you, lady. Satisfied? Good! Here's your two dollars back, plus a two-dollar profit.''

The pitchman disposes of the five lighters in a like manner, but adds a dollar each time he makes a transaction. He now has maybe a dozen ''live ones'' who are ready to ''participate'' in his ''advertising program.''

"Here's Twenty Dollars
for Buying That Ten-Dollar Watch"

Do you remember my mention of the "shills," or "sticks," who moved through the crowd to encourage them to move into the tent? Sticks serve another function; they start the action—the "bidding"—if the customers (or "marks") don't jump to the bait rapidly enough. By now you may be wondering how you can make money by giving the customer his money back every time he buys something. Well, you can't! So, sooner or later, the pitchman has to make his move. The stick helps him to do this. Here's how it works. The pitchman picks up, say, a lady's wrist-watch.

"I'm going to pass out four of these ladies' wristwatches. Who'll give me ten dollars for one of these watches?" A lot of hands go up, *including* the hands of the two or three confederates (sticks) in the crowd. The pitchman hands a watch to one of the sticks. "Here's your watch, sir. Give me ten dollars." The stick gives him ten dollars. The pitchman goes through the same routine as before, asking if he's satisfied, giving the money back, giving the stick a ten-dollar "bonus" for "participating." Of course, you will realize that any transaction made with a stick is a bogus transaction. But nobody in the crowd knows this. The transaction *looks* and *sounds* like other transactions. To all appearances, the pitchman is not only refunding a customer's ten dollars but is giving him a ten-dollar bonus, plus a wristwatch! Even if the watch doesn't work, the customer (or so it would seem) will have made ten dollars on the deal. At this time there will be perhaps twenty people with *greed,* if not *larceny,* pounding through their vascular system. The pitchman quickly passes out two more watches, this time for twenty dollars each, and this time (secretly, of course) to confederates. Again he gives the money back, again he gives a "bonus."

Now comes the "blowoff," as it is called. This is the moment that all this buildup has been leading to. The pitchman holds up a watch. "Who'll give me twenty dollars for this last watch?" If the pitchman has correctly gauged the moment and the tip, there will be perhaps fifty hands raised for the one watch. He is right. At least forty hands go up. He acts surprised. "Whoa," he says. "I've only got one watch. All right—here's what I'll do. I was supposed to pass out the rest of these watches later in the week. But you folks have been so nice that I'll go ahead and distribute them now. But we'll have to move fast so we can get rid of this other merchandise." He waves his hands at the stacks of merchandise behind him. "So get your money ready, and hold it up where I can see it." A forest of twenty-dollar bills appears. The pitchman starts passing out watches and snatching twenty-dollar bills. Within five minutes he has passed out maybe forty or forty-five watches and has taken in $800 or $900. Can you guess how many people get their money back this time?

"Thank you very much, ladies and gentlemen. You've been super. We'll be passing out more merchandise in about an hour from now." And that was it. The wholesale cost of the watches, direct from the importer? Would you believe $3.00?

This has been a long lesson. Unlike the other lessons, it is not really a "how to" lesson. (I hope you don't take it as such.) However, it should teach you much about human nature that will be of value to you. If all it does is to press home an understanding of the incredible power of aroused *feeling* in a selling/buying relationship, it will have done its job.

LESSON NO. 65: DON'T GET CAUGHT IN THE HEAT OF YOUR OWN FIRE

Fear as a Motivator

There is no question that *fear* is a powerful selling motivator. Most of us like to think that it is prudence and caution that motivate us to buy insurance for protection against losses due to fire, sickness, or death. But caution and prudence are intellectual activities. They do not press against us and compel us to act. To be cautious is to rationalize the unreasoned and deeply unconscious fear of danger or loss.

Many salespeople find that clients are more easily motivated to protect what they have than they are motivated toward gain. What one has is *real*. What one may acquire, whether property or profit, is only *possible*. This is partly what makes selling the challenge that it is. It takes some doing to get people to exchange something real for something that is only possible, however probable it might be. Appeals to fear are more effective when applied to something prospects have than when applied to some future benefit which they might miss out on. Which is to say that your prospects are more likely afraid of being without the money it will cost for your product than they are afraid of not getting the profit, not getting the convenience that your proposition promises.

Playing with Fear

There is danger in inducing fear that goes beyond the strength needed to induce prudence and care. Strangely enough, low-level fear is a more powerful motivator than high-level fear. During World War II American servicemen were shown movies which depicted in graphic detail the possible consequence of sexual promiscuity. Contrary to what one might believe, showing pictures of persons who had been ravaged by venereal disease *did not* reduce the incidence of such disease among service people.

Similarly, educational efforts that were loaded with high-fear messages concerning the danger of cancer did little to reduce the amount of tobacco consumed prior to the government ban on television commercials promoting cigarette smoking.

Psychologists now believe that the reason high-fear messages fail when low-fear messages succeed lies in the basic optimism which most people feel. When a contingency is presented in such a horrible manner as to shock the sensibilities of a normal person, *there is an innate tendency to deny that it could happen "to me."* The high-fear condition creates such tension that there is a pressing need to remove the tension, a need that is so strong that it most often can only be satisfied by immediately removing the tension. So the mind simply sees the condition as happening to "somebody else."

The Power of Negative Thinking

You face another danger if you constantly use fear as a motivator; the danger of what I call *psychic infection*. Selling has its physical aspects in the delivery of merchandise, service after the sale, billing, and so on. But it is primarily a *mental* activity. The sale takes place in your mind and in the mind of your prospect before there is a transfer of property. So what happens in the mind can be of vital importance—not only to the sale you are working on, but to future sales as well. It might be well for you to review Lesson No. 7, on learning to "dehypnotize" yourself. If you stay in selling long enough, you will discover that your clients affect you just about as much as you affect them. You cannot call regularly on the same people without developing a symbiotic feedback loop. The mutual dependency that this loop engenders requires trust, faith, and confidence—not fear.

LESSON NO. 66:
THE EMOTIONAL APPEAL OF COLOR

Package Your Proposition in Color

There was a time when business was done in black and white. Telephones were always black. Typewriters were black. Men wore black suits and starched white shirts. Women (when they "intruded" themselves into the business world) wore black dresses, starched white blouses. Everybody wore black shoes and black stockings. If you drove to work, it was in a black car. Business letters were *always* written or typed in black ink on white paper.

Read the above paragraph again. How does it make you feel? It makes me feel as though I've just come from a funeral. We are truly blessed by our Creator in our ability to see the world in color, for many of the earth's creatures do not so perceive it.

Color is a most effective nonverbal communication tool. The language of color is a rich one, and its nuances can only be hinted at here. Color speaks directly to our emotional nature, by passing the intellectual left-brain processor and going straight to the subliminal processing centers in the right hemisphere of the brain. Some colors seem peaceful and relaxing; others, invigorating and exciting. Bright red and orange-yellow are well known for their attention-compelling value. Besides individual and personal color "meanings," there are cultural color meanings. While black, in our culture, is a sombre and "dignified" color that is often associated with death, in some cultures *white* is the color of mourning!

You'll need to do some personal research to arrive at a good understanding of this subject, but you can begin at once to use color more effectively in your presentations. For example, there is really no good reason to use *only* white paper in your written proposals. Experiment with stationery now available at most office-supply stores: papers in light beige, oyster, pearl, ecru. Most modern typewriters permit use of colored ribbons. Try brown, blue, or green for variety. Even red is good for emphasis, if it is not overdone. It should be remembered that color is more useful in headlines and in short passages of "body copy." If your proposals cover several pages, large blocks of type should still be in black for legibility.

Color Photographs Sell

One of the most effective uses of color in selling is the use of color enlargements. Audiovisual presentations are great, but simply not practical for many propositions and for many selling methods. If you are making many quick calls in a day, you really don't have time to set up a projector and screen. Even if you use the small self-contained projector that shows the picture on its own built-in screen, you need more set-up time than many propositions permit. Color enlargements offer a viable alternative to regular audiovisual equipment and a much cheaper alternative, too.

You can take the pictures yourself with any good 35mm camera. A series of eight by ten enlargements inside of plastic sheet protectors, bound in a three-ring binder, will make a strong visual backup for any sales talk. If your product is not a colorful one, be sure to add color to the props in the picture. For example, a rather drab piece of machinery might be seen sitting on a piece of red velvet. Or someone wearing colorful clothing could be in the picture.

Business Cards Can Be Colorful

Ask your printer to show you a variety of business cards that have been done for others in color. Consider two-color or three-color cards. Look into the new four-color process cards. If you are near a large city, you'll find prices much more reasonable for four-color printing than in small cities. Some printers offer a business card with a full-color photo on one side and printing on the reverse side. The photo can either be your own photo or a photo of your product. Most printers can handle full-color business cards or post cards at a lower price by jobbing out your work to some large, "gang-run" color printer. The "gang-run" method combines several orders for similar work on one press run. Be sure to ask about "gang-run" prices when you start shopping for color printing. And don't take the first price you get—you'll find a wide range of prices for the same work.

If you do your own photography, here's a final tip. Use a wide-angle lens for your product photography; it will give you greater overall sharpness, as well as make a more dramatic presentation. There will be some distortion, especially in close-ups, but experiment with this and you will be pleased with the results.

LESSON NO. 67: BUILDING WORD-PICTURES WITH EMOTIONAL PUNCH

Explore the Power of Adjectives

Adjectives add color and warmth to verbal presentations. Yet few sales-people bother to use adjectives other than "great," or such hackneyed adjectives as "economical" or "cheap." Maybe there'll be a "fantastic" or a "terrific" thrown in for good measure. Rarely will you hear an adjective with real descriptive power behind it. Perhaps you remember an earlier suggestion concerning a book called *The Word Finder*, by J.I. Rodale (Rodale Books, Emmaus, Pennsylvania) and another book by the same author and publisher, called *The Synonym Finder*. Use these two books together in building your next sales talk, and notice how much more emotional force your words have. The power of these two books lies in their thoroughness and organization. For example, suppose you were selling a "pegboard" accounting system to doctors' offices. You want a synonym for the word *system* and find such words as *process, procedure, method,* and *technique.* Next, look up any of *these* words in *The Word Finder,* where you will find several adjectives—words like *flexible, innovative, effective.* Get a sheet of paper and make two columns. In the first column, write the synonyms for your original word. In the second column write the adjectives:

process	flexible
procedure	innovative
method	effective
technique	

You might easily have thought of those words without looking them up, but follow the explanation anyhow; perhaps it will whet your appetite. Once you start using these two books, you will find that they stimulate your thinking processes so that you can make more effective word combinations.

Now go back to the two columns of words. You can see that it is an easy matter to combine a word from the second column with a word from the first column to create a more vivid and a more vigorous description of your proposition. Instead of referring to your pegboard as a "system" every time you mention it in your presentation, you call it a *process*—a *procedure*—a *method*—a *technique.* And by combining these words with the describing adjective, you can say something like, "This innovative procedure provides you with a truly flexible means for. . . ." The next time you mention this, you could say, "Here is an effective technique to. . . ."

Keep Your Prospect in the Picture

It is easy to get so wrapped up in your product that all you want to talk about is the product. There is an easy way to avoid that. Make a resolution right now to begin every new thought with the word *you.* To take my own advice, I'm going to restate one of my own thoughts. "This innovative procedure provides you with a truly flexible means for . . ." (above) will now become "*You will appreciate* the way this innovative procedure provides you with a truly flexible means for. . . ." Probably this is somewhat strained and artificial. Granting that, I still suggest that you form the habit of doing this until you are sure that all of your word-pictures include the most important component—the customer.

Keep Your Word-Picture Shows Short

It is almost impossible for your prospect to sustain a high level of emotional interest in your proposition for prolonged periods. Many books on selling advise you to build rather complex scenarios which depict the client enjoying the product. It is probably true that some masters of the art can get people to sit still for a ten- or twenty-minute word show, in which the client is shown doing all sorts of enjoyable things that he could only do if he owned the product. But the real, live sales pros whom I have talked to all tell me the same thing: As soon as you sense a high degree of emotional involvement, you'd better try for a close. Emotional tension begs for release. A closing question provides the vehicle for that relief. And that's the subject of the next chapter.

6

Everything You Always
Wanted to Know
About Closing
But Were Too Busy
Talking to Ask

Is there a magic moment, a certain psychological "ready state," that exists in the mind of your prospect and that makes a close possible? And what if this "moment" is missed? or passed? or fumbled? Does it come again later in the presentation? or is it forever gone? Expert closers have long argued these points. Almost all agree, however, that there is only one way to *be sure* when it is time to close: Close early—and close often. The three dozen or so closes detailed in this chapter will help you to do this.

LESSON NO. 68: FIVE STEPS TO WARMER COLD CALLS

This lesson is probably one of the most important in the book. That is why it is placed in the beginning of the most important chapter, this chapter on closing. A cold call is a call that is made for one reason, that of walking in unannounced to make an instant presentation and secure an immediate buying decision. You can't use it under all conditions, nor with all propositions. But where it is appropriate, it is the most powerful selling and closing technique you can use. Here are the five steps.

1. *Skip the formalities.* Don't introduce yourself. Start talking about your product or service at once. Skip the small talk. Pull some strong benefit of your product or service out of the middle of your presentation, and open your cold-call presentation with this benefit. Say something like, "Probably every salesman who comes in wants to help you save money. You know that what they're really here for is to *get some of your money for themselves*. However, I know that if I can show you how to eliminate losses you now incur from hot checks [or employee theft—or faulty wiring—or whatever your proposition protects against] YOU will take care of the money saving yourself. Here's what I mean. . . ." Then go into your presentation. This approach catches them off guard.

2. *Hand the prospect a sample.* The surest way to prove that something you think you see is "real" is to reach out and touch it. It is difficult—maybe impossible—to really prove that anything is so. But the more of our five senses that agree on anything, the more convinced we are that it is true. We confirm the evidence of our ears by looking and touching. Your prospects hear you and doubt at least half of what you say. When they *see* a picture or a drawing that confirms what they hear, they doubt a little less. When they touch something that confirms the evidence of their eyes and ears, they believe much more.

3. *Leave your business cards in the car.* When prospects ask for your business card early in your presentation, they are telling you to go away. If you hand cards out at this point, don't be surprised to hear, "We'll call you when we need something." And you may be sure that your card will be dropped in the trash can before the door has closed on your heels. Yet ignoring a request for a card would be rude. Your only safe way out of this dilemma is to say something like, "Of course. I'll get you a card out of the car before I leave. By the way, may I have one of yours?" This will put the initiative back in your hands where it belongs. Many prospects ask for your card because they're not yet interested in your proposition and consider it impolite to just tell you so. If your prospect hands you a card at this point, look at it and read the name aloud. To get back into the rhythm of the presentation, try this: "Miss Jones, thank you. I'll file this away for future reference. Please don't let me forget to give you one of mine before I leave. However, before I go, there is just one thing I feel you'll want to know about . . ." and continue with your presentation.

4. *Stick to business.* There is no time to "visit" during cold calls. If you have made four or five calls in a row without arousing interest in your proposition, it is easy to take these turndowns as personal rejections. And if you're feeling rejected, you may be really ready for a friendly face or a warm, kindly voice. Don't be sidetracked. You may well have run into the kind of person who likes everybody, even salespeople. You must be ever on guard against things that steal your time. Be aware that the overly friendly person who throws you off by talking about everything except your proposition is rejecting that proposition just as much as if he or she had slammed a door in your face. Keep trying to bring the conversation back to the business at hand, and if you can't do that in short order, *leave.*

5. *Close often.* Too many salespeople treat cold calls as "missionary calls." Make no mistake about it, it is possible with most lines to close the sale on the first call. But no matter what you think the situation is with your particular proposition, *you will never know for sure unless you try.* CLOSE EARLY AND CLOSE OFTEN!

LESSON NO. 69:
THREE TRIAL CLOSES THAT WORK

The Nature of the Trial Close

Beginning salespeople sometimes hesitate to use trial closes. Some feel that such closes are "tricks" which can force a customer to buy something that he or she doesn't want to buy. Put all fears from your mind. These closes *will not work* if you haven't done your job. If you have not attracted attention and sustained interest long enough to arouse a strong desire to possess your product, and if you have not *convinced* the prospect that the purchase is justified, these "closes" will not trick anybody into signing on the dotted line. However, if you have first done all that you should do, a psychologically sound trial close can curtail procrastination and move the vacillating prospect to do what he or she really wants to do—NOW.

Close No. 1. The decision on a trivial point. A prospect hasn't said, "I'll buy it." Neither has she said she won't. Certain mannerisms suggest that she has accepted the proposition; she keeps picking up the sample, jotting down numbers, looking at the spot where the equipment would be installed. Whatever signal you get, ask this question:

Our delivery date will be a week from Saturday. Will that be soon enough?

Close No. 2. A choice between something and something. Again, you are reasonably sure that your prospect is ready to buy. If she answers this ·question at all, she has to answer it in an affirmative manner. She may, of course, in this and the other trial closes, simply ignore your question. Here's a sample question:

Shall we send this in the sand beige, or would you rather the dark grey?

Close No. 3. The assumed assent. One last time: You should at least *suspect* that your prospect is ready to buy. The best way to describe this close is to tell you to just start writing. To use this close effectively you should have the orderbook out very early in the selling process. From the very beginning, the prospect sees it and so is not shy when you start to use it. The question:

May I have your shipping address?

Or, while looking at a the customer's business card, with your pen poised:

Is this the correct billing address?

Objections after a trial close. Since trial closes are designed to discourage a "no" response, the prospect has to use some other semantic device to answer you in the negative. The usual form this negative response takes is *the objection.* Objections should always be treated as requests for more information. Briefly acknowledge the objection— paraphrase it and "play it back" to the prospect. Then give him or her some more reasons for buying, and try another close. Skilled closers often have three or four "something or something" closes and as many "trivial-point" closes committed to memory. You will probably use the "assumed assent" close only once in a selling session; it is such a powerful close that to use it several times would smack of high pressure.

Silence and the Put-off. Because of the way in which trial closes are worded, prospects sometimes use two other devices to avoid answering them. A common device is silence. Silence will usually trigger more "selling talk" for an amateur: It shouldn't from you. (More about silence in the next lesson.) Silence should be countered by silence. Wait for an answer. The second device is the lame put-off. The prospect wants to "think it over." Respond with, "Certainly. And while you're thinking about it, consider this . . ." Give more reasons, and end with another trial close.

LESSON NO. 70: THE POWER OF SILENCE IN CLOSING SALES

Silence Is More Than Listening

Courses are being taught in many large cities in something called "creative listening." Perhaps you have attended such a course yourself. Listening *is* important. And paying attention to what prospects and clients are saying is vital. But you also need to know how to induce the "thoughtful silence" in a prospect's mind—and you need to know what to do about it when it happens. An understanding of the meaning of the thoughtful silence is difficult to convey by means of a theoretical discussion. A couple of dramatizations should help to clarify this important concept.

The "Good Talker"

This first story tells about a situation in which a long-time direct salesman found himself. He was selling a product called "The-Ten-For-One Collection System." The "system" was actually a group of collection letters which bore the letterhead of a "collection agency," but which would in fact be mailed directly to the past-due accounts by the professional person, hospital, or other direct-credit grantor. The designers of the "system" had worked out a powerful one-call presentation which Frank Petrie, the salesman, had rehearsed so many times that he could deliver it without it sounding "canned."

Frank had called on a prospect who owned a large pharmacy. The man told Frank that he had several thousand dollars in past-due accounts. So Frank kept trying to sell him. The prospect listened. Frank tried for a close several times, but instead of answering the closing question, Frank's prospect simply remained silent. He never said yes, and he never said no. Finally, "good talker" though he was, Frank left (without a sale) so that he could deliver his sales talk to a more responsive prospect.

The Good "Waiter"

Frank Petrie mistook his prospect's silence for reticence, so he was never able to harness the dynamics of this silence. When you have made a really effective presentation and have reached the moment of closing, you will probably test for a close with several closing questions. It is at this point that the "thoughtful silence" has a chance to develop in your prospect's mind. And it is at this point that many salespeople ruin their chance of making a sale. They don't know how to wait.

Jerry Stansburry is a good "waiter." Jerry sells ID plates to manufacturers of small machinery. He has learned something about inducing the "thoughtful silence." For example, he had narrowed down one customer's choice so that he was looking at four different designs—even though he hadn't committed himself to buying anything. When the time came for the close, Jerry asked a question like, "Which of these four designs do you prefer?" No answer. Jerry waited. And waited. In total silence, he waited. It seemed like an interminable wait, but at length the customer said, "Give me 4000 of this oval design."

The Dynamic Tension of Silence

When you ask a customer a question which requires him or her to make a choice, a tension is set up in the mind that can only be relieved by the customer reaching a decision and giving you an answer. This is the "thoughtful silence." If *you* break into this silence with more sales talk, you dissolve this tension and dissipate its power as a decision-making and sales-producing force. There is only one way to make this power work for you. Wait.

LESSON NO. 71:
THE "ASCENDING-COMMITMENT" STRATEGY

A Boon for the Cautious Client

Ascending commitments help your cautious clients to make more "reasoned" decisions. This strategy can help you to feel more comfortable about closing, too. This is especially true if your sales personality is not as "dynamic" as you think it should be. Sales reps who really enjoy a more aggressive stance are probably more at home using stronger closing techniques—closes that rely more heavily on persuasive skills. We'll go into some of those later on.

Suppose that your client is feeling more suspicion than interest in your proposition. This suspicion will usually be expressed in the form of certain challenging questions. You make a statement, the prospect challenges it. As soon as you accept the challenge and "prove" your point, the prospect has another challenge. If you continue in this fashion, your prospect or client will be guiding the course of the sales interview. Very often, cautious or suspicious clients simply want the opportunity to participate in the process. They are only suspicious of decisions which seem to come from the outside, rather than from their own reasoning.

Planning Your Questioning Strategy

There is a superficial relationship between the "trivial-point" type of question (see Lesson No. 69) and certain initial questions used in the "ascending-commitment" strategy. However, the ascending strategy consists of a *series* of carefully planned questions, each one more important than the other. An employment counselor who sells various employment services to executive job-seekers used the "ascending" strategy this way.

Some of her clients want to talk about being burned by other counselors. She has learned to cut in gently by saying something like, "I'd like to hear more about that just a bit later. But, let me ask you—would you like to see what we have done to prevent this from happening here?" Of course, the answer is usually in the affirmative. She then proceeds with her presentation. Her next question might be something like, "Does this sound like a program that would work for you?" Each question will require a slightly stronger commitment.

Here are a few sample questions. You should have little trouble framing some of your own after looking these over:

1. If you were convinced that our $1000 printer would last four times longer than our competitor's $500 printer, would our price seem more reasonable to you?
2. May I show you the results of engineering studies which compare our machine with that of our competitor?
3. If you are convinced by the results of these engineering studies that ours is the best buy for you, will you reevaluate your decision to buy our competitor's printer?
4. Does this material convince you that our printer is the best for you?

Closing after the Ascending Commitments

With a little imagination this strategy can be adapted to fit any proposition. However, I need to make one last comment on this technique. These are "trial closes," not *arguments!* If you haven't done a good job of *selling* your proposition, neither this nor any other strategy will "close" a sale that hasn't been made. If this strategy is introduced into the presentation too early, your prospect may very well be *convinced* of the merit of your product, but will still not *want* it. If this happens, it usually means that you have failed to arouse your prospective client's emotions. He or she doesn't *feel* a compelling need for your product or service. The tip-off in a case like this is a comment something like, "I'm convinced your printer is best. When we get ready to buy, we'll certainly give you a shot at it." You'd better take "a shot at it" now. People forget.

LESSON NO. 72:
ASK EACH QUESTION TWICE

They Almost Never Say No

Maybe you've noticed it yourself: Your clients and prospective clients almost never give you a flat no. Usually, they will say, "Try me later." Or, "Maybe after the first of the year." Sometimes it will be "Check with me the next time you're in the neighborhood." Perhaps I should qualify this. People will frequently tell you they're not interested if you ask for action before you've really given them reasons for buying. But if you really put your heart into your presentation, most people feel that it is impolite to just give you an out-and-out turndown. Still, put-off *means* "no" if you accept it. YOU can convert it into a *yes* with this simple strategy.

First, agree with your prospect. Suppose you've tried to close at an appropriate spot in your presentation, and the client says, "We're overstocked now. Check with us next time you're around." You say, "Sure. Be glad to. By the way, something you might want to be thinking about in the meantime is. . . ." Go back into your presentation. After you've given more buying reasons (NOT necessarily reasons for buying now, just more buying reasons), ask the same question again. As incredible as it may seem, people will often respond positively the second time they are asked.

There Are at Least Two Ways
to Ask the Same Question

You get more mileage out of a question if you reword it. There are at *least* two ways to ask every question—and probably two hundred or two thousand would not be an exaggeration. For example, let's suppose you have just asked a question like, "Would five dozen of these be an adequate starting stock?" The client says, "We're overstocked right now. See us on your next trip around." You give some more selling talk—*not talk which overtly addresses the issue of buying now versus "next trip," just more buying reasons; more benefits*. Then you come back with the same question in slightly different form: "What would you say? fifty or sixty of these?"

The Same Words Mean Different Things

You might think that speaking a common language assures that two people mean the same thing when they use the same words. 'Tain't necessarily so! This is another reason for asking a question again in different words. This is also the reason why it is sometimes wise to repeat a statement about your proposition in different words. Another person may even have negative meanings for words you use in a positive sense. It is also possible that your listener *heard* a certain word, but because of a hearing impairment didn't catch your *intonation*. Here's another thing: We can review *written* communications if we miss something, but spoken words are just hot little breaths, quickly uttered and, often, soon forgotten.

Don't forget the really important part of this strategy. No matter what your client says to put you off, *agree first*. Then give more benefits. Then—and only then—*ask again*.

LESSON NO. 73:
"HIGH PRESSURE" CLOSING

Exactly What Is "High Pressure"?

There is often a fine line between high pressure and just good salesmanship. Since we are not just salespeople, but sometimes are customers too, I suspect we each have our own ideas about when "good" selling becomes "high-pressure" selling. However, I make these important distinctions:

> *Good* salespeople pile on *benefits,* backed up with *features* that prove those benefits.

> *High-pressure* salespeople attempt to "persuade," rather than to demonstrate.

> *Good* salespeople are persistent.

> *High-pressure* salespeople are insistent.

> *Good* salespeople will make several calls to close without offense, if that is necessary.

> *High-pressure* salespeople rarely make callbacks. So what if they offend? There are plenty more people to call on!

High Pressure and the Naive Buyer

There was a time, not too long ago, when a great deal of emphasis was placed on getting a customer to sign a contract. Older books on selling are full of strategies which involved such devices as handing the customer a pen at a "strategic moment." You will read about such devices as tipping the orderbook up and rolling a pencil down it so that the client will grab the pencil. Presumably, the client will also grab the orderbook out of your hands and push you aside so he or she can sign the order! It is my belief that such a gimmick can work as well as any *if the customer is ready to buy anyhow*. If the customer is ready, you can roll a pencil across the desk, or you can say, "Just sign here," or (as one book suggests), "Press hard, you're making a carbon copy." It won't matter in any true business *relationship*. But if you have not taken the time to establish these relationships, none of these strategems will really work over the long haul. Today, it is only the naive buyer who thinks he can't get out of a deal he was pressured into. And it is only the naive sales rep who thinks a buying contract can be enforced just because somebody signed something.

Will It Get Cold During
the Cooling-Off Period?

Truth-in-advertising and truth-in-lending (or financing) laws have done much to protect buyers from the old bait-and-switch high-pressure tactic. You will probably recognize this as the tactic wherein a cheap, advertised item is "nailed to the floor," so to speak. The salesperson would show it to you with a total lack of enthusiasm. Then he or she would ask, "Did you see the other ad?" You'd, of course, respond with "No," since there wasn't any other ad. The salesman then showed the higher-priced item and really turned on the steam to sell it.

To my mind, there is nothing wrong with switching customers to higher-priced merchandise, so long as the cheaper item was fairly advertised and was available at the advertised price.

There are several possible honest applications for this switch technique. For example, an auto dealer could have a customer use a "loaner" which would be a later model car, while a "bargain" car was being checked out by the shop before delivery. Similarly, a typewriter salesperson could offer an old machine at a bargain, but deliver a newer machine "temporarily." There are countless *softer* ways to use these old hard-sell, high-pressure closing methods. There is nothing basically wrong with the method, so long as there is never the *intent* to be anything but fair and honest. One successful salesman was quite open with his customers about his use of this tactic. "Your machine won't be ready till next week," he'd tell them. "In the meantime, maybe you'll fall in love with this new machine. If you do decide to keep it, I'll give you credit for what you've paid on the bargain machine."

LESSON NO. 74:
THE CLOSE BY DEFAULT

The Free-Trial Close

There are all sorts of things that can be sold using this close. The beauty of the close is that it doesn't require the customer to do anything. On the contrary, it is the very inertia of the customer that closes the sale! Perhaps this close works best with those customers who are more conscientious about keeping the promises they make. However that may be, countless sales are "closed" simply because some customer neglected to exercise an option to return merchandise left on trial.

To make the default close work, there needs to be a definite understanding as to when the "trial" becomes a sale. Probably the best way to handle this is to bill the customer on the first day that the merchandise is installed "on trial." Terms should be the usual commercial terms of net, ten days. The bill should contain a provision that it may be paid either by return of merchandise or payment in full by the tenth day following invoice date. It is important that the customer understand that after the ten-day trial period, the merchandise may not be returned for credit. The object of this strategy is *not* to trick anybody into buying unwanted merchandise. You will still have to do all of the usual things you do in making a sale. The trial, however, helps to clinch the sale with a customer who is really *sold* but has a natural tendency toward procrastination. It enables you to *use* this very procrastination to close the sale.

The Telephone Follow-Up

Be sure to follow up *no later than the fifth day* on all trials you have out. This is usually enough time for your prospect to get past the difficulties caused by initial strangeness of the equipment and is still far enough away from the "default date" that you have time to correct any negative condition. Give the prospect everything you have on the fifth, sixth, and seventh days if you have to, but get lost after that. Under no circumstances should you call the prospect at or near the tenth day.

Small-Ticket Defaults

Probably you are more accustomed to thinking of free trials in terms of "hard goods," such as office machinery and appliances. The principle will work just well on fast-turnover "soft goods." A salesman selling nutritional products—vitamins, weight-control and dietary aids—uses the *default close* to good effect. While the principle is the same, the method is slightly different. Obviously, once a package has been opened he cannot resell it. So he furnishes a small sample package of the product (a "ten-day supply" of vitamins, for example). The customer is to try the sample first. If the sample is not satisfactory, the large package remains unopened, and the salesman picks it up at the end of the trial period. There is another difference in using the default close on these small-ticket sales. Some people don't feel responsible for the safe return of such merchandise—especially if isn't satisfactory. One way to solve this problem is to collect for the product in advance, with the promise of a "no questions asked" refund if the customer tries the accompanying sample and doesn't open the large package. However, fears that you will lose money on these small-ticket trials are probably unwarranted. Book clubs have long used this method of closing sales. So have companies catering to stamp collectors.

LESSON NO. 75:
THINK "CLOSE" ALL THE TIME

Developing the "Closing" Mindset

The close begins before you even meet with your prospective client. It begins in your own head. Top closers are people who understand that learning how to "think positively" about selling means learning to see yourself *closing*, not thinking in terms of a certain sales volume. You need to set dollar goals, true. But until you are totally free of the fear that often comes at that moment of truth—the close—you will need to concern yourself more about *what you do* than about *what happens*. Don't concern yourself with results. Do what you are supposed to do, and the results will take care of themselves. Close early and close often, and sales will come as a consequence of your action. Don't wait to check this out before committing yourself to total acceptance and belief. Accept this statement as one of the maxims of selling:

> Concern yourself about what you do, not about what happens. Concern yourself about what you do, and the results will take care of themselves.

Why Should the Prospect
Believe What You Doubt?

If you have fallen into the habit of thinking of the close as a definite, well-marked step or spot in the sales process, you will doubtless feel a sense of apprehension as you approach that spot. When closing is viewed from this perspective, it is difficult to feel easy or loose about it. Many salespeople begin (and end) their sales careers believing that they've learned selling, but not closing.

If you fear closing, your mind may subconsciously try to "save" you from what you fear by constantly pushing the closing moment into the future while you pile on more sales talk. Ironically, you may find yourself getting better and better at delivering the facts of your proposition while you are making fewer and fewer sales. One garrulous young sales rep of my acquaintance sells "preneed" cemetery lots. His delivery is beautiful, and it is packed with tremendous emotional appeal. Although I have long believed that cremation is the only civilized way to dispose of the dead, I changed my mind several times while listening to him. But the point was really moot—he never got around to asking me to buy. And I was too fascinated with his presentation to interrupt him.

Convince yourself of this fact: *Many of your prospects are ready to buy almost at the very beginning of your presentation.* If you close early—*very early*—you will save yourself countless wasted hours and dramatically increase your sales. But if you doubt that your proposition is such that an early close will work, you will likely convey that doubt to your prospects. After all, why should they believe what you don't?

"Affirmative Action"—A New Perspective

What if you *don't believe* that you can close early? If you don't believe that an early close will work, my simply telling you to believe is like saying that the cure for poverty is to get some money. Or telling a barefoot man that he need only wear shoes to solve his problems. It is what philosophers call "arguing in circles." Yet, the cure for disbelief *is* belief! Many people find that it is possible to replace doubt with belief through the use of *affirmations*. Try it; it may work for you. Simply say over and over to yourself:

> *I know that many sales will practically close themselves if I will simply* ASK A CLOSING QUESTION.

The exact words you use aren't important. The important thing is that you say these words over and over, many times a day, until you believe them.

LESSON NO. 76:
THE "BIG T" CLOSE

"Let's Look at Both Sides"

This close is strong in logical appeal, and it is a good one to use on prospects who seem on the verge of buying, but need just an extra "kick" to get them to act. To use the close, pull out a clean sheet of paper and, with a bold felt-tip pen, make a big capital *T*. As you do this, say, "I don't blame you for hesitating. You impress me as the kind of person who isn't comfortable without examining all the pros and cons. Let's look at both sides of this question." Next, under one "arm" of the *T*, write a major benefit of your proposition—say, "Saves money on paper." On the other side of the *T* write some offsetting *disadvantage*; perhaps something like

"Slower speed than nearest competing machine." Maybe the second benefit would be "Immediate, local service." The corresponding disadvantage could be "Higher cost for service contract." Keep this up until you have perhaps four or five benefits and at least three disadvantages. Then, as though it were an afterthought, list another two or three benefits. Again as an afterthought, list another disadvantage. When you have done your work, you will have maybe nine or ten benefits and probably three or four disadvantages.

Encourage Prospect Participation

Prospects and clients are always impressed by your frank admission of a disadvantage. By inviting prospect participation, you further enhance this feeling of fairness. A good way to get the needed participation is to ask a question like, "What other good reason can you think of for *not* buying?" If you get another reason, write it on the negative side of the *T*. Then ask, "Can you think of another reason why this proposition might be *right* for you?" Since this doesn't require a strong commitment, many prospects will give one or two positive reasons. Some, once they have broken the ice, will think of *several* reasons—even some you haven't mentioned. Certainly, the best sales are those that customers make to themselves.

The "Big T" has been around for a long time. Sometimes it is called the "T-Account" close, after a device used in accounting to test balances. Sometimes this close is used in a way that suggests that one side of the *T* is a credit, the other side a debit. But I saw a twist on this old device that made something new out of it. The salesman using the "Big T" in the manner I have described it always drew his *T* so that the first arm started lower on the page than the second arm. In other words, the top bar of the *T* was slanted *upwards*. Try to visualize this before continuing. Better yet, draw a *T* in this fashion. Make it large enough to fill the central portion of an 8½ × 11 sheet of paper.

As I said, this salesman drew his *T* this way before he started listing his benefits and disadvantages. When he finished, he quickly drew three lines down from the top left of the *T*, then sketched an oval at the end of the three lines. He did the same thing on the other side of the *T*. With just a few quick lines, he had converted his simple *T* into something that looked like a set of scales. Of course, the *left side*, where he had listed his benefits, appeared to be pulling the right side up, as if outweighing the right side of the "scale."

Just a simple bit of business; yet a powerful nonverbal way of saying "These *benefits* far *outweigh* the disadvantages." Then he would hand his "scale" to his prospect, followed by one of his closing questions.

LESSON NO. 77:
THE FINAL-OBJECTION CLOSE

The Buildup

This is a good close to use right after the "Big T" of the previous lesson, since the *T* will often smoke out a hidden objection—one that your client has been holding back for one reason or another. Unfortunately, some people have the uncanny ability to say "no" without feeling the need to give a reason for such a reply. While you never want to get into the trap of answering one frivolous objection after another, you will certainly want to answer any *real* objection that your client raises.

Whether you use the *T* or not, to use the "final-objection" close you will build up to the big objection by asking for any negative reasoning that is holding the prospect back. Write these objections down as the client gives them to you. Most of them will be minor, and you may want to ignore them. However, if you persist, your questioning will usually elicit the "big one," the really important objection that is standing in the way of the sale. Do some real thinking about this objection. Try to get the prospect to talk about it so that you are sure it is the objection you are looking for. Make sure that you have the answer to this objection before you ask your closing question. Double-check like this:

Besides this, *is there anything else* standing in the way of a deal?

Nailing It Down—Questions
That Encourage Truthful Answers

Asking direct questions encourages direct—but not necessarily truthful—answers from your prospects. Friends may simply say to each other, "I don't want to do it." Acquaintances (prospects, customers, clients, tradespeople, co-workers) often find it more comfortable to lie! How do you get them to tell the truth? Easy! Make it more comfortable for them to tell the truth. In asking for their "disadvantages," be careful to create the impression that you are on the way out—that you have given up. You're throwing in the towel, and you just want to know why your prospect has *decided not to buy*. If the prospect feels that you are seeking "objections" that you can *answer,* and thereby continuing trying to sell, you may not get a truthful answer. One way to handle this is to close your attaché case and to make preparations to leave. While doing this, say "By the way—what's your *biggest* reason for deciding against this?"

The Ultimate Commitment

Memorize this question: "If I can solve this problem for you, do we have a deal?" It is important when you ask this question that *you* are ready to follow through. The nature of the question implies a *reciprocal* commitment. A sincere prospective client will think carefully before making such a commitment. "Yes" to your question means "yes" to the sale. But "no" makes it sound like the stated "final objection" was a lie. Clever maneuver? Maybe. But you're dead if *you* renege!

LESSON NO. 78:
THE POWER CLOSE

After Several "Almost" Closes . . .

While many closing techniques can be applied almost anywhere in the sales process just to test for closing readiness, this close is *always* reserved until you are convinced that you have exhausted all of your selling ammo, and you feel that the prospect is ready to become a client. The time to use this close is after you have tried several closes, with the prospect "almost" buying a couple of times. It is strong medicine, best reserved for inveterate procrastinators and similar miscreants. This close depends on pure persuasive power for its effectiveness.

"Your Profit Will Be Continuous"

Let's say you've been working on the sale for half an hour or so, and the prospect seems sold, but keeps trying to put you off. Try this: "Mr. Prospect, let's say that you and I are both involved in an effort to make more money. Of course, I don't deny that if I conclude this sale, I will make an immediate profit. My profit, however, will be small when it is compared with your profit, which will be continuous, since it will come to you for as long as you continue to use this product.

"Your reason and judgment are satisfied; your deepest feelings tell you that this is the sort of thing you ought to do. You know that your judgment is your court of last resort. And you know that any time you fail to act in accordance with your own good judgment, you fail to serve your

your own best interests. You simply fail to do yourself justice."
Pause.

"If you were my own brother, Mr. Prospect, I'd say this to you:
Buy this." If he still vacillates, continue:

"Really, Mr. Prospect, don't hesitate. He who hesitates in the face
of a sure and certain course of action deprives himself of countless benefits in life. Okay this contract now, and you will have the satisfaction of
knowing that you have done the right thing by yourself. You will have
really served your own highest interests."

The Emotional Appeal to Reason

This close is an old one, and it is not much used today. It is a rather blatant use of raw emotional power. It stresses the importance of abiding by
one's sense of justice to oneself; it appeals to the faculty of judgment—
but the appeal is an emotional one. To use this close effectively (and it is
a truly effective close), there are three points that you must keep in mind:

1. Only use it after you have tried several other closes.
2. Only use it when you are convinced that the prospect is sold, but simply is
   procrastinating.
3. Only use it if you have *thoroughly learned* it, and you are *completely comfortable* with it.

LESSON NO. 79:
THE "SWEETENER" CLOSE

The Only Time to Close Is Now

You probably don't like the idea of giving "discounts" in order to make
sales. Much of the traditional selling wisdom advises against such discounts. Call it what you will—discount or price cut—there is something
positive to be said for it, too. If you can *close* today—now—instead of
tomorrow, how much money will you save? Isn't it worth it to figure a
way to pass some of this savings on to your client as an incentive to
move? Probably you will have to think of some way to justify cutting the
price. For example, if you have quoted a price of $2000 on a piece of
equipment, then you drop the price to $1500 for a quick close, *you* will

feel somewhat uneasy about it. Will the prospect think it was really *overpriced* by $500 to start with?

The Present Value Versus
the Future Value of a Sale

In the fast-moving world of high finance, it has long been understood that a bird in the hand is worth *at least* a bird and 10 percent in the bush. Understanding the *present value* of money over the value of the same sum at some date in the future is the very basis of finance. Why isn't this true in sales? Believe me, it is. With the profit from a sale you've made today you can perhaps pay the rent or a car note. At least you can buy dinner for yourself and a friend. What can you do with the commission on the sale you *might* make tomorrow? Of course, you may not have the leeway you need to use this kind of close. Your employer may set iron clad prices which you have no choice but to follow. Where you are allowed some discretion, however, there are several things you can do to "explain" the discounted price.

One salesman kept a running total of sales made to date. His commission on sales made after a certain quota was far greater than it was before the quota had been reached. He used this fact to give him some maneuvering room. Another rep made sure that he heard about "cream puff" repos as soon as they came in. If somebody else sold the repo before he could get it, he'd go ahead and deliver a brand-new model for the repo price, taking the cut in his commission. When he made delivery on a deal like this, he explained, "Somebody beat me to the repo. Here's a brand-new model; I'm taking the loss out of my commission."

"If the Office Approves This,
Do We Have a Deal?"

One of the cleanest ways to justify a discount in the eyes of your prospect is to call your office. If you can get "permission" from anybody, and I mean literally *anybody,* this somehow seems to take the onus off the transaction. I once worked with a sales rep who had, at one time or another, called nearly everyone up to and including the firm's president to secure "permission" for a price break. He tells me that he sometimes had trouble with the janitor, but other than that no one had ever refused him. Before calling, he always boxed the client in by asking, "If they approve this, do we have a deal?"

Bring in the Brass

Some people are terribly impressed by the voice of authority. The very same deal coming from one higher up may sound better to them. Quite aside from this, however, it is quite possible that your sales manager will see or hear something in the situation that you have overlooked. If nothing else, bringing your sales manager with you can give you a good excuse to make just one more attempt to close a difficult account. And there is one other angle. Nobody wants to look like a numbskull in front of the brass. That's true for your client, and it's true for *you*! It's just possible that you will do a better job of selling while your sales manager is present, just to show that you can do it. Want to check this out? Carry your tape recorder with you, and check the tape you make against some you've made when your manager wasn't with you.

**You Be the Sales Manager for Me,
I'll Be the Sales Manager for You**

Auto dealer salespeople have been known to use this device, and a very effective one it is, too. The sales rep does everything possible to close a deal first. Just before the customer walks out, he says, "Just a minute, please. This is the best deal I can make you, but let me get my sales manager. Maybe he can do better for you." Then he gets another person, who comes on with a better price. Later, with different customers, the roles will be reversed.

The Second Chance

The sales-manager close offers you one way to "solve the problem" mentioned in Lesson No. 71. It may very well be the kind of close to use on those objections for which there doesn't seem to be a solution in the usual sense. For example, if the prospect complains of a lack of funds, you may have no possible way to solve this problem. In the strictest sense, it may also be that your sales manager can't solve that kind of problem either. However, just the *presence* of the sales manager can be enough to alter the conditions that seem to make up the problem. Maybe the prospect can now speak from a different kind of feeling. Maybe there is a different sense of rapport with this new person. It is even possible that a new feeling can encourage a more creative *outlook*. Maybe the client will think of resources not considered before. Maybe he will see that he *can* afford to buy.

Following Up on the Sales-Manager Close

If your introducing your sales manager does change the dynamics involved so that the prospect now feels he or she can buy, then you have, in a very real sense, solved a problem for that prospect. However, if there is to be a good continuing relationship after the sale, it will be necessary for your sales manager to pass control of the account back to you in some very obvious way. The customer should never be thinking that this has become a "house account" as a result of the sales manager's having assisted in the sale. It is usually enough for the sales manager to remind your customer that you will be coming around to make sure everything is okay with the new installation, and so on.

LESSON NO. 81:
THE ANECDOTAL CLOSE

One Good Story Deserves Another

Everybody loves a good story. If you can tell a story that shows how a customer enjoyed your product or service, or a "before-and-after story," you can easily tie the end of the story to a request for an order. Think about some of the sales you have made in the past. You may have to wrack your brain a bit, but I know you can come up with *several* good stories if you really try. Some of the material for this book comes from professional salespeople I have interviewed over the years for Prentice-Hall's Bureau of Business Practice publications and for other business publications. Many of the people I've talked to tend to talk in generalities until I insist, "Tell me a story. Tell me about something that happened. Tell it in the past tense." *Always,* if I persist, my subject has been able to come up with a story about how he or she sold something, how the customer liked it, how the customer was able to solve a problem, etc. If you consider yourself a *communicator,* I know you can tell stories. When you finish the story, convert it into a close by saying something like, "That's the way they used my product. How would *you* use it? What do you think it will do for you?"

The Success Story

You may be selling for several years before you accumulate several good success stories. But start collecting them now. There are all sorts of stories that could be considered success stories. However, I'm suggesting that you start looking for stories in which the subject has achieved something noteworthy. Perhaps this has not been totally as a *result* of using your product or service, but if you will dig into the matter you may very well find some interesting connections. Let's say you read about some small business-person who installed a certain automated process. This makes the local news. Clip the news story, and check it out. Does this firm also use your product or a *similar one*? Contact them and ask them about it. You may be able to build a good story here. If you can, you can combine *your* story with the one in the newspaper. Also, you can ask your employer for names to follow up on for these kinds of stories. If your employer has been in business several years, the chances are good that there are a number of such good stories floating around. Remember to close with a question like, "I think you know that successful people like this don't buy or replace such equipment lightly. May we install this on a trial basis to see what it will do for *you*?"

The Failure Story

Like the success story, the "failure" story takes some seeking out. Failure stories may not make the news, yet they may still be strong enough for your purpose. Again, ask your employer for stories about a customer who (say) persisted in using antiquated or worn-out equipment to "save money," until more efficient competition moved in. Close with: "May we help you to avoid this?"

LESSON NO. 82: LETTING THE BOSS SELL THE BOSS

You May Be Barking up the Wrong Tree

Some "buyers" won't admit that they don't have the authority to buy. It is not that they are totally lacking in authority; just that their authority is limited to being able to say "no." Some so-called purchasing agents *never* initiate an order for merchandise or equipment; they simply execute the purchasing requests which come from department heads, or from the

CEO, or from somebody else. Of course, there is nothing wrong with this system, but you need to be aware of it, or you may waste countless hours "closing" the wrong person. It is also possible that a department head will not have any real authority to buy or even to effectively recommend a purchase. You may be able to save yourself a lot of trouble by asking a simple question: "How do you get these people to buy you what you need?" You may get an answer that will tell you what the situation is; perhaps one like, "Oh, they let me have anything I ask for." Or, "They're pretty tough, but if I can show them I need it, they'll let me buy it." On the other hand, if the answer suggests that buying authority is totally in the hands of someone higher up, you may have to call in *your* boss, or an "expert" (could be just another salesperson) to change the relationships. You might even ask the department head (or whoever), in a somewhat conspiratorial manner, "Do you think my sales manager could convince your boss?" If you do this right, you won't offend your no-authority "buyer."

Setting It up "Between Bosses"

Never let your no-authority "buyer" feel that he or she is about to become superfluous. Your attitude should be one of constantly seeking help. Just make a comment now and then such as, "I really do appreciate your help in this. I know your CEO [or whoever the real buyer is] depends heavily on you department heads to furnish the information needed to make informed buying decisions."

You may now be tempted to seek to make your own contact with the *real* buyer. Of course, you can always do this if you have to. However, it may very well pay you to continue with this relationship for just a bit longer. If you have sold this person on the merits of your product or service, you have a real ally when the time comes to close the real buyer. And there is one other angle worth noting: Competitors of yours who are just coming on the scene may be foiled by this same no-authority person. It is even possible (if you play your cards right) that this will be done *purposely,* as a "favor" to you!

Keep the No-Authority "Buyer" Involved

Regardless of your expanded effort to reach and sell the *real* buyer, continue to call on your junior contact and to apprise him or her of new developments. Be sure that when you show up with your sales manager, you introduce them to each other. Make a comment like, "I want you to meet somebody who has been a real help to me. If it hadn't been for him,

I'd still be floundering around trying to figure out who to talk to."

LESSON NO. 83:
THE "START-WRITING" CLOSE

Write Early, Write Often

The surest way to overcome what I call "Orderbook Block" is to begin writing almost at the very start of your presentation. By the time you are ready to write the order, your client (and you) will be so accustomed to your writing things down that it will be totally comfortable and natural for you to write the order and close the sale. Lay out your writing materials— your pen, a notepad, your orderbook—right at the beginning. Take copious notes while your prospect is talking. Make notes of what you learn about competitive products, about objections, etc. When the time for the actual close comes, start writing in your orderbook. If nothing else, sign your name and write the date. And quit thinking of those pristine, neatly numbered pages as though they were valuable. Don't be afraid to void an order form if you have to. Your employer won't mind when your closing ratio zooms!

Let's Work This Up

Learn to write your proposals in the form of an order, using your regular order form. After you have made your presentation, nothing could be more logical than to just go ahead and write up a "suggested" order. As a matter of fact, it really works well if you put it just that way: "Now here's a suggested beginning order for this merchandise." And go ahead and write the order. Or you can say, "Let's work this up and see how it looks." Either way, when you have finished, hand the order over with a pen.

It's Not a Contract Unless You Sign It

Some prospects seem surprised that you should expect your presentation to lead to an immediate sale. The anatomy of the sales process is a complex one. It is probably safe to say that most of your prospects (especially in cases where you initiated the call) believe that they are considering a proposition that they will act on at some time in the future. This is probably true even when they are buying everything you are telling them about your proposition. It is often only at the very last that the realization comes to them that there is every reason to go ahead and make the commitment *now*. Writing the proposal up in the form of an order, on your regular order blank, is one of the cleanest ways to bring everything to a head. Some prospects will watch you write a contract and then look it over *still* with the thought in mind that this is something they are deciding on for the future. Sometimes they will say, "Why, this is a contract!" A reply that gets action is, "Not unless you sign it!" Be sure the prospect is holding a pen when you say this.

A Word of Caution

Beginning salespeople who watch the "writing close" for the first time miss an important factor. While you will start writing early in the presentation, it is only after you know you have done a good selling job that you try to close in this fashion. Try to write up an order like this prematurely, and it will backfire. This is the difference between *selling* and high pressure.

LESSON NO. 84:
CLOSING WITH A TAPE RECORDER

Sometimes, Informality Works Better

In Lesson No. 9, "State-of-the-Art Selling," I mentioned the use of a microcassette tape recorder in place of an order book. Whether or not you can do this in your operation, you should try the tape recorder as a closing tool. The essence of closing lies in *action*—some action on your part which causes a sudden shift in the thinking of your client. The shift is from thinking of your proposition as something about which he will have to make a decision "sometime," to something about which he must make a decision *now*. This shift will rarely happen by itself. As mentioned earlier, you will usually have to do something to force the decision. It really doesn't matter what your action is: You may write an order or a "proposal" that has to be acted on. But if you reach for your tape recorder at just the right moment, you can accomplish the same thing. If you feel comfortable doing this, it can be even more effective than writing an order. It is the novelty of it, and the informality of it, that does the trick. The only real difference is that you "start talking" in this close instead of "starting writing."

Here's an example of how it works. You would say, perhaps, "Let's see. You prefer the beige color? And the model XB should be just about right for your needs, wouldn't you say?" You might get an answer like, "Well, if I got anything, it would probably be the XB." You say, "All right—and would you prefer the large screen or the small?" Your client might answer, "Probably the small." Now you pick up your tape recorder and turn it on. Speaking into it, you say, "Let me make myself a note of that. XB—beige color—small screen." Look at your client and ask, "Did I get that right?"

Just Tell Me What You Want, I'll Do the Rest

The tape-recorder close works especially well for salespeople selling many small items, such as tools, shop chemicals, janitor supplies, and job merchandise. Some buyers seem always to be in a hurry and will often say, "I need a few things, but I don't have time to give you an order right now." It's easy to close this type of buyer with the tape recorder. Just say, "I heard that. I can see you're busy. Just tell me what you need, I'll write the order later." If there will be a lapse of several days before delivery, you may want to protect against your verbal order getting "cold." Do this by sending a written confirmation of the tape-recorded order.

Purchase order numbers? They're usually needed if your merchandise is going open account. But if the merchandise is accepted and signed for on delivery date, you shouldn't have a problem.

LESSON NO. 85: THE TELEPHONE-CONFIRMATION CLOSE

The Touch of Urgency

When you get telephone confirmation of inventories, changing prices, delivery schedules, etc., your client appreciates the importance of acting now. This works especially well where you have quoted a special price to get quick action. Remember, the whole point is that you have initiated some new action that wasn't called for by the normal flow of your presentation (as far as your client could see). Never forget that the client is thinking "someday," while you are thinking "now." Here's what happens when you use the telephone to "confirm" a special price.

Let's say that your prospect hasn't really jumped at the special price. Here's how you introduce a bit of urgency into the situation. Say something like, "You know, that price came down about three days ago and only for a limited number of units. Maybe I'd better check on it. May I use your phone?" When you come back, you could say, "We still have one at the price. I told them I promised it to you." If your prospective customer says nothing, follow up with, "We'd better go ahead and firm this up before we lose it." Pull out your order blank and "firm it up" unless you're stopped.

Checking for Special Deals

Closely allied to the price-confirmation close is this strategy. The difference here is that you have tried to close without dropping the price; then, as a last resort, you say something like, "We may have a repo, or seconds, or something that has been scratched in shipment. These are hard to get, and they go out about as fast as they come in. And no wonder. Who wouldn't snap up a bargain that saves one-fourth to one-third of the price? I'll check and see if we have anything. May I use your phone?" If the prospect doesn't discourage you from making the phone call, this is a good sign of interest. Just remember, it's up to you to close on this showing of interest.

On Being Overheard

Be sure that your prospect is within easy earshot of your conversation. As soon as you get the confirmation you're looking for, say in an animated voice, "We *do*? Great." Then, looking at your client, say, "Send that out to [name your client] at . . .[to your client] what's this address?" *Don't hesitate. If the client does nothing to stop you, proceed as though you have been told to place the order.* You can always cancel the order if you have to, but if you do this with confidence, the chances are excellent that you will close at this point.

LESSON NO. 86:
LET'S GO TO LUNCH

Quit Trying to Build Good Will, and SELL!

Thousands, perhaps millions of dollars have been squandered by naive salespeople in the hope of creating "good will" through the medium of the business lunch. Get this: You can't cram, stuff, poke, or even tease enough food down the gullet of an uninterested prospect to create enough good will to offset that lack of interest. Neither can you offset the merits of a competitor's product with food. But you can *sell* during a business lunch. Buyers *are* often more receptive during lunch than they are just before or just after. There is an important point here that is often overlooked, however. *It is during the actual eating of the meal that people are more susceptible to persuasive ideas.* So, no matter what your mama told you, you may have to talk with food in your mouth! Here's a really hot tip: Encourage your prospect to eat heartily, but you eat lightly so that you *can* speak gracefully while eating.

The Quid Pro Quo

Suppose you are just on the verge of going for the close, and lunch time overtakes you. If you have done a good selling job, a good line is, "Let's wrap this up over lunch." Your prospect hasn't made a commitment, but by accepting your offer in this way a *quid pro quo,* or a "something for something" obligation is suggested. The price of the meal may not be important if the meal is *special.* One salesman knew the whereabouts of all the "working" people's restaurants. Most were famous for supergenerous portions of simple but really delicious food. He had taken the same buyer to lunch in a different such restaurant on each of several occasions. At the last such lunch, she said, "Jack, I'll be glad when you wrap this deal up so you can quit trying to impress me."

Of course, such plain surroundings and simple (no matter how generous) fare will negatively impress the supersophisticate. You have to know your people. Likewise, if the restaurant is *too* posh, it may seem as though you are offering a bribe. Don't be surprised if an insulted prospect even grabs for the check (or at least his check) and spoils everything.

Foiling the Check-Grabber

There is a simple way to make sure that your potential client doesn't embarrass you by paying his own check. A few minutes before the meal is finished, quietly excuse yourself. While you are away from the table, take care of the check, even if you have to leave enough extra to cover last-minute additions.

LESSON NO. 87:
THE CONTEST CLOSE

The Customer Contest

Some people are totally unaffected by contests. Others are motivated almost as much by what they *might* get in return for a purchase as they are by any number of sure and certain benefits. For them the element of chance offers excitement, stimulation, relief from boredom.

Because most states have rather strict laws concerning any kind of contest *requiring* a purchase as one of the rules of eligibility, it wouldn't be wise to attempt to tie your contest to purchases. You may remember what we said earlier about the *close* of the sale being a matter of instituting *action*. Take a tip from the national magazine promotion which, it is claimed, makes millionaires of lucky winners who simply *send in* the winning application blank—with or without a purchase of magazine subscriptions.

The Salesperson Contest

The elements of excitement and suspense that motivate people who like contests will often work even if it is the *salesperson* who stands to win instead of the customer. When people like you, they want to help you— even more so if they can do this while helping themselves through the benefit your product confers.

Since initiating action is the purpose of the contest, you will need to tie the customer's action to something that the customer signs, or at least fills out. This might be only a "request for information" packet, or a "put me on your mailing list" form. Most people using this strategy only mention the order blank as an official contest entry form—at least until such time as the sale looks hopeless. At that point, the salesperson pulls out the "request for information" form, which still gives the prospect a chance of winning (without having to make a purchase).

By the way, many sales contests in which the salesperson is the big winner provide that any prize from a *drawing* be awarded in duplicate; one to the customer and one to the winning customer's sales rep.

I'd Like to Take This with Me to the Sales Meeting

Since the purpose of the contest is to initiate action *Now* instead of later, almost any "excuse" can work as a contest does, so long as it provides the element of suspense. One sales rep tells her customers how her sales manager announces the name of the person making the biggest sale each week on a moveable sign out in front of the store. She says, "I think this sale will put me over the top this week." And it frequently does. Another rep tells how his sales manager awards a trophy each week. "I'd like to take this order to the sales meeting, if it's okay with you," he says.

LESSON NO. 88:
THE "BLAST-OF-HEAT" CLOSE

The Magic Seven

You cannot name seven real benefits without naming at least two or three that will appeal to almost *any* real prospect for your proposition. Throughout your sales presentation you have endeavored to direct your presentation so that you can hit targeted emotional hot spots you have reason to believe are right for your prospect. Yet, you have reached the point where you should be able to close the sale, and you still run into strong resistance. Why? Who knows! Maybe you were wrong in your assessment of what will motivate this particular prospect. It doesn't really matter now. The important thing is that your "rifle" approach has not worked. No matter how accurately you have fired, there is no prize for getting a bull's-eye on the wrong target. Perhaps what you need is to shoot at *all* the targets on the range. For this you will need a *shotgun* approach. This closing technique fires a blast of heat in such a broad spray that *all* of your product's emotional appeal is delivered in one last blast.

Make a List and Memorize It

The power of this close depends not only on the power of each appeal, but on the cumulative effect of all seven appeals delivered in quick succession, with total dedication and with intense fervor. Put everything you have into this effort. You will not be able to do this if you have to stop and think. Why *seven* appeals and not five, or eight? There are several reasons for this. Not the least of these reasons is the human preoccupation with the number seven. There are seven days of the week. Philosophers have said that children reach the age of reason when they are seven years old. The age of puberty was thought to be at fourteen, and the age of maturity at twenty-one (multiples of seven). Early Christians talked about the "seven sacraments" and the "seven deadly sins," and all sorts of other sevens. Our fairy tales are full of sevens: Blubeard's seven wives, the seven keys, the seven dwarfs, the seven-league boots.

While we don't consciously worry about all these *sevens* today—in fact, we consider it a lot of superstition—you shouldn't forget that you are not dealing totally with the *conscious* mind when you use emotional power. The emotional right half of the brain is still very much steeped in the symbology of an era not yet gone by. So when you say, "There are seven reasons why you may want to reconsider your decision," your prospect's emotional right brain says "Seven? I'd better listen."

You Can Do without This Product,
But Not without These Benefits

Your Magic Seven benefits should be such that, even if your client doesn't buy what you are selling, he or she will try to secure them in some other way. You need to make your client see that your proposition is the best *present source* of these benefits. For example, suppose you are selling a home-security system. By the time you are ready to use this closing technique, you have long ago convinced the prospect of your product's technical superiority. So you shouldn't even be talking about the *product* at all by now. If your prospect is a husband and father, you will be intensifying his natural protective instinct with appeals such as this: "You've lived in this city long enough to know that *while we are talking,* somewhere in this city, somebody is *right this minute* breaking into an unprotected home; perhaps one like yours. Perhaps a child or a wife is being beaten or killed, *this very minute.* If I could talk to the father of that family I wouldn't have to convince him that he should have had this system. I know you may not feel the need for the nuts and bolts, the wires and circuits in this system. But I am just as sure that you do want the safety, the security, the freedom from fear that it will give you and your family. I know that you want these things so strongly that if you don't buy this system you will still try to secure these benefits. You will try to secure freedom from fear, perhaps by far less effective means. Some people do this by simply denying that the danger exists. Others pray. Some attempt to convince themselves that they have the raw physical power to protect themselves and their families. . . ."

Perhaps this particular example is a bit too long or a bit overdrawn. With the power of your voice behind it and delivered with a certain intensity of feeling, you could probably express the same thing with half the words. If so, so much the better. Since you will want to build seven such little talks, you will want to economize a bit.

Eventually, Why Not Now?

Your "blast of heat" is directed to the task of convincing your prospect that, sooner or later, he is going to see the wisdom of buying your proposition. Announcing your "seven points" creates the impression of a closed system which exists as an eternal verity. There is a vast psychological difference between information that is delivered in this fashion and the *very same* information presented as though you were "thinking it up" as you talked. When you present your closing arguments with such obvious feeling and authority, and following a preannounced plan, you enlist the aid of several powerful teaching and convincing techniques. Your client will almost surely feel that, even if he *can't* act on your proposition now, sooner or later he will!

Here are the important points to remember about using this technique. First, announce that there are *seven* important reasons why, sooner or later, your prospect will demand the benefits provided by your proposition. Quickly name these seven benefits, with feeling and authority in your voice. You will need to know them as well as you know how to spell your name or recite the alphabet. Next, give your "blast of heat" for each of your seven points. Last, mention the seven points again, and ask a closing question.

LESSON NO. 89:
THE BLOCKBUSTER CLOSE

Drop Something You've Been Holding Back

Dropping a "blockbuster" can open a closed mind and close a lost sale. The principle behind this method is a subtle one. The blockbuster may be something added to the deal, like a special price, an extra piece of equipment, or special terms. Or it may be a benefit conferred by a new use for the product. However, the thing that makes this close special is not the "extra," but the fact that this "extra" has really been a part of the proposition from the very start, but you have deliberately refrained from mentioning it. Ideally, the blockbuster will not look like something that was tacked on to close the deal, but rather something that is freshly perceived as a benefit which *justifies* the purchase.

The Proposition Must Be Strong
without the Blockbuster

A baby-stroller salesman sells a marvelous piece of "safety furniture" that is beautifully designed to make up into a high chair during infancy and to convert to a table and chair as the infant becomes a toddler. Everything is handsomely done in chrome and laminated plastic, and he does a good job selling just the two pieces that make up into the two kinds of outfits. He has worked out several strong closes for mothers of newborn children. However, he has noticed that some mothers think more about the *immediate* utility of the outfit. So he withholds the fact that there is also a *set of wheels* which attaches to the underside of the chair, so that the outfit includes a *stroller* as well as a high chair and (later) a youth chair and table. Thus he has a *blockbuster* which he can drop to close difficult sales.

An important point to remember is that the proposition must be made as strong as possible *without* the blockbuster, or the blockbuster will just seem like another benefit. You should be able to close many, if not most, of your sales *without* the blockbuster. That is to say, you should be able to close most of your sales without *mentioning* the blockbuster, since it is part of every deal anyhow. This strategy keeps you on your toes, since it forces you to add as much value to your proposition as possible before giving the client all the "hardware" he or she has coming.

The Value-Added Blockbuster

If you have been selling for some time, you have probably come to understand and to appreciate the "value-added" concept. That is, you have learned that selling is not just a matter of talking somebody into buying something; it is also a matter of your *adding value* to your proposition. Sometimes you do this by educating your client to new uses for your product. At other times you may add value by showing extra features and benefits that may never have been discovered without your help.

Think of some of the ways in which you add value to your product or service by arousing a feeling of admiration for it and for what it will do. You also add value when you "create" a body of customers for the product, customers which would not be there except for your efforts. The more people *desire* an object, the more *valuable* it becomes. Thus you can drop the value-added blockbuster by creating a strong desire for some benefit that is not *immediately obvious* in your proposition, and then, at the critical moment of closing, show how your proposition not only fills other needs, but also *unexpectedly* fills the need that you have "created" or intensified.

A good example of this would be dropping "teasers" into your presentation to continually amplify or heighten a need while showing how other needs are met. For instance, if you were selling computers, you would demonstrate how to do bookkeeping, filing, spread sheets, etc., while only briefly mentioning word processing, even though the client is obviously interested in word processing. Of course, to make this work, you would have to give a really masterful presentation of the points about which the prospect seems not to be interested. If you work it right, you should be able to build and intensify the interest in the benefit which you have been "withholding" to such a point that it is a real blockbuster when you drop it.

LESSON NO. 90:
TELL A GOOD STORY

Make It One They'll Never Forget

When using a story to close a sale, you'd better make it a really memorable one. Otherwise, forget about using it. Study the anecdotes you use in your anecdotal closes (Lesson No. 81). Which of your anecdotes can be expanded into a real story? Need your story be the literal truth in every regard? You'll have to decide this for yourself. It has been my experience, however, that most accomplished storytellers rarely let the truth get in the way of a good story. Whatever you decide about this, you will certainly want to keep the nucleus of your story truth—especially when you are talking about real people. You would not, for example, tell a story about some real-life customer who could be identified without being accurate in the important details of the story. Certainly you would never claim or imply that some identifiable person is a customer of yours unless this is the literal truth. Even within these confines there is much room for poetic license, however.

A Good Story Must Stress a Telling Point

For your story to lead naturally into a close, it must have a high degree of relevancy to some telling point that you have just made or plan to make just before asking your closing question. Go back to Lesson No. 11, and reread the short story I told concerning the memory system that I once helped to promote. The point that I made by this story was that such "systems" sometimes did not produce lasting results, and that what I proposed required a better understanding of the way our memories work. Then I "closed" by telling you that the solution lay in *rehearsal,* and in carrying a "name book" until names were committed to long-term memory. As you examine the story I told in Lesson No. 11, you will realize that the short joke that I tacked onto the end of the story is not literally true and is not even part of the story.

Yet the joke reinforces the point made in the story and gives the story much punch. Old-time salespeople frequently told jokes simply to entertain customers. I never tell this kind of joke when I am trying to sell.

Jokes should be used only when they help to move you closer to an important point. Tagged onto the end of a story as I have done here, the joke echoes and emphasizes the point of the story.

Never Assume That Everybody Gets the Point

It might rightly be said that a joke (or a story) isn't very effective if you have to explain it. Yet, no matter how good the story is, *somebody* will miss the point of it. There may be a play on words or on meanings that depends on a common culture or upbringing to be understood; an intelligent person from another background may totally misunderstand (or fail to appreciate) what is meant by certain veiled references that normally make a joke funny. For this and other reasons, you should always end your story with a restatement, in straightforward prose, of the point of your story. You needn't be so obvious as to say anything like, "Now the point is . . ." That would be insulting to some people. But you can say something like, "This is why I strongly suggest . . ." Then move right into a closing question.

Put Your Prospect in Your Story

As time goes on you will learn several good stories. If you are careful to tell stories in which the main character is clearly similarly situated to your present prospect, the story will have far more cogency. Some sales trainers advise that you learn to construct stories which depict your prospect enjoying the product. For example, a real estate agent attempting to sell resort property might say something like, "Just picture you and your family coming here after a hard week in the city. See yourself diving into the crystal-clear waters of this lovely lake. . . ." And so on. Perhaps you can do this effectively. Most people who try it become uncomfortable with the out-and-out playacting required to pull it off. When you tell a *real* (albeit dramatized) story about *real* people who are like your present prospect, you can count on the prospect to project himself or herself into the title role. With richness of detail, warmth, and color, your prospect will see the scenes and feel the action just as much as if the story were being told from his or her point of view. When you ask your closing question, you can safely assume that the prospect is seeing and feeling your story as though he or she were in it in the place of your hero. Thus, you may ask a closing question such as, "How do you like it? What days of the week will your family use your property most?"

The Playback Technique

Learn the art of paraphrase and multiply your closing power. There are many times when an adversary wants as much that you *understand* him as he hopes that you *accept* his point of view. While a customer is not an adversary, an *adversary relationship* does often develop when a customer raises an objection which is not answered satisfactorily. You should realize that there are many times that objections cannot be so answered. And there are times when even *trying* to answer them can lead to trouble. But you will never get in trouble by showing that you *understand* your client's point of view, even if you say nothing about how you feel regarding it. For instance, your client may say, "Your product is way too high for my budget. I will have to get along without it. Maybe my method is old-fashioned, but at least I won't go into debt using it."

If you have arrived at the point where you should be able to close the sale, you sure don't want to get into a protracted argument about the several points that a complex objection is likely to raise. So here's what you do: Nod your head. Say, "Let me see if I understand your position. You feel that our product is too high for your budget, so you're going to go ahead and keep using your present method. Do I have that right?" When your prospect agrees that you have correctly paraphrased him, thank him and give another strong benefit of owning your product or using your service. Or go into one of the closes like the "blast of heat" (Lesson No. 88).

The Unanswerable Objection

Once you have gone through your sales presentation, most objections fall into the "unanswerable" category. Frequently, such objections are simply a last-ditch effort on the part of the prospect to delay making a buying decision. Here are some examples:

Objection: "I like what you have, but I want to talk this over with my wife (husband)."

Answer: "Let me see if I have this right. You're satisfied, but you'd like to talk it over with your wife. Right?" After confirmation, say: "You might also want to mention this point to her . . ." Go into a blast-of-heat close and again ask a closing question. If you do a good job with "blast of heat" or one of the other closes, your prospect will likely forget about "talking it over." Here's a similar objection:

Objection: Sounds good, but I need to think it over."

Answer: "Let me see if I have this right. Everything is clear, but you need some time before you make a decision. Right?" Upon confirmation, come back with, "I understand. By the way, while you're considering this, you may also want to think of this additional information; it should help you to make a more informed decision." Again, you would go into one of the other closes, like "blast of heat," then finish with a strong question that offers a choice between "something and something": "We have this in either grey or beige. Which would go better in your office?" Or you might say, "Our regular delivery date is on the twenty-fifth. Will that be soon enough?" Remember, no matter how "clever" your paraphrase is, you need to end with a restatement of benefits and a question.

LESSON NO. 92:
REOPENING A CLOSED MIND

"Before You Make Your Final Decision"

Memorize this phrase: *Before you make your final decision.* Nothing reopens a closed mind like the subtle suggestion that the case has really not been closed. Save this one to use after you have been given a definite "no" and there doesn't seem to be any way to reverse it. Be ready with some pretty strong stuff after delivering this phrase, because you *will* get one more crack at it. Whether or not you can keep your prospect's mind open depends on what you do next, and it had better be good.

This is also a good strategy to use when your prospect says that he or she has decided to buy your competitor's product. You needn't be unduly alarmed by such an announcement. Many people are motivated most by the last impression they receive. If this is the case, you will have ample opportunity to get back in the running with a fresh presentation. Just remember the magic phrase, "before you make your final decision."

Do the Groundwork by Paraphrase

Sometimes, upon being told that a competitor has beat you out, you will need to do a bit of groundwork *before* trying to reopen the sale. The *paraphrase* device mentioned in Lesson No. 91 is the thing to use. Say, "Let me see if I have this straight. Bonzo Company is offering you a dozen of these fittings for the same price we've been getting for ten of them, and since your company has instituted its new economy drive, you can't pass up the savings. Right?'' After confirmation, say, ''I'd probably do that too, if I believed I was getting the same thing for less money. Before you make your final decision . . .''

Acknowledge Your Competitor's Benefits

All top pros that I have met know as much about their competitor's products as they do about their own. Most of them feel that there is really no ''best'' product in an absolute sense—that there is rather sometimes a ''best'' under certain conditions or for certain purposes. So, most often, it is not really true that your competitor's product is a better buy. Yet your prospect may have good reason for believing that it is. When you learn to acknowledge these reasons, it becomes much easier to reopen a mind that has been closed by your competitor. Here's how you use the paraphrase technique to acknowledge your competitor's benefits:

''You've been looking at the Boffo machine, and you're impressed by it, aren't you? Well, I am too. I especially like the styling of the Boffo, and its speed and quietness. Did the Boffo salesman tell you that the Boffo machine is used in the White House? It has some advantages over our machine, no doubt about it. Before you make your final decision . . .''

How to Make Comparisons that Lead to a Close

Your prospects will be impressed by your thorough product knowledge. They will be even more impressed if that knowledge extends to your competitor's products. Perhaps your company has prepared comparison charts which show the relative advantages and disadvantages of the various competing products alongside yours. If they have not, it may be worth your while to prepare such a chart (or charts) yourself. At any rate, you should be prepared to do your own point-by-point comparison with any competing product in the marketplace. Often you will find that making this comparison will convince the prospect that a choice between two products is really a tossup, and the purchase is more logically made on the basis of which *salesperson* to buy from, rather than which *product*. Now it truly becomes a matter of selling *yourself,* and if you can do this, then it is no longer a matter of comparisons at all. Just one more good closing question, and the sale is yours!

LESSON NO. 93:
SAYING NO IS JUST A HABIT

Getting the No's Out Early

Get this into your head before you start, and it will save you a lot of grief during the day: Nobody don't want nothing from nobody! It's your job to change that; this is the very reason why salespeople are hired to hustle sales, and if it weren't for this fact, your product could be sold through a giant coin-operated machine. So thank God that this is the way things are; if it were otherwise, you wouldn't have a job.

Every prospect you will meet during the day is primed to say no to whatever question you ask. You will hear in some quarters that you should start your customer saying "yes" as soon as possible. You will be advised to ask questions like "Nice day, isn't it?" Answer: "Yes." "Isn't it great how much time these new machines can save?" Answer: "Yes." "Isn't it wonderful how you don't have to be rich to drive a new can in this country?" Answer: "Yes."

Supposedly, once your prospect is in the habit of saying "yes," he or she will say "yes" to an important question when it is asked. I don't believe it. I don't believe that you need to *encourage* them to say "no," either. But you do need to give people the opportunity to speak their minds early. Ask pertinent, not vacuous, questions. Let them get their no's out early. Some really intelligent people will back into a stubborn stance if they are prevented from expressing their minds early in an exchange.

How to Spot the Habitual No-Sayer

The kinds of questions you ask will determine the kinds of answers you get. You are trying to close a sale from the moment you begin talking to a prospect. Why ask insipid questions about the weather, or about business, or about the economy, or about baseball teams? If you want to see what kind of person you are dealing with, ask closing-type questions. Ask closing questions right from the start. Almost everybody will answer your first question with a no. But the no-sayer won't elaborate. She doesn't feel the need to explain, since she says no to everything, all the time—unless you give her a really good reason to say yes. If the prospect explains, you probably don't have a habitual no-sayer, but, have instead an ordinary nice person who would rather say yes but doesn't feel justified in doing so. These people don't want to hurt your feelings, so they explain in the hopes you will understand. Of course, your job is not just understanding people, but making sales.

Leading the No-Sayer to a Close

People do not continue to respond against their own self-interest. If you suspect or discover that you are dealing with a naturally contentious individual, it is important that you permit this person several early "wins." To do this without damage to your presentation, save your heavy stuff until later, when the no-sayer will have less need for self-expression. You can then softly lead to your important closing strategies by saying something like, "You have apparently given this much more thought than most people do. I can see that you are quite knowledgeable in this area. Before you make your final decision . . ."

Beware of the Too Early Yes-er

As bad as the habitual no is the too-early yes. Prospects who agree too early often are doing so out of politeness. These early yeses are totally meaningless, but they are not harmless; few things can so effectively kill valuable time. When you suspect you are getting polite but meaningless yeses, push for a close. You will find out in a hurry where you stand. Far better a truthful no than a string of yeses leading nowhere.

LESSON NO. 94:
THE "WHAT-ELSE" CLOSE

What Else Can I Do for You?

Your prospect may not be interested in the benefits you are offering, but may feel a need for something else. Why not give him a chance to express this need? You may think that your proposition is such that if you can't fill the prospect's needs with the product you are offering, then you can't do business with him. That's tunnel thinking. You are thinking in terms of your particular proposition rather than in terms of helping a particular prospect. Maybe you need to join a service club such as Kiwanis or Rotary or the Junior Chamber of Commerce, where you can meet other salespeople so you can trade names and leads. Every prospect you meet needs help from *somebody* in solving a business or personal need. It is really possible, with this shift in thinking, for every call you make to result in a closed sale for somebody you know. Think about it.

What Can I Add to This Sale?

No matter how large the sale is, *always* try to add something else to the order. Your total sales at the end of the year will show a dramatic increase without any additional work if you will do one thing. Think of the investment you and your firm have in each call you make. There is your time, first (probably the most expensive item). Then there is your traveling expense. Any sale that you tack on to your main sale, in effect, rides free. If your firm doesn't have such tack-ons that you can sell, you may want to explore the possibility of brokering some item on your own (if this is permissible). Of course, if you are an independent, there is no problem. Whatever the case, be sure to check out swapping leads with salespeople handling other, noncompeting lines.

What Else Can My Product Be Used for?

You can sometimes close a sale by discovering (or inventing) another use for your product. Think about your proposition from this angle. Do some real hard thinking. Spend several hours at this; the results may astound you. Imagine your product used in outlandish ways and for preposterous purposes. Write down all the ways you can think of. Suspend judgment until you have listed at least twenty different ideas. Then look over your list carefully. You may have one or two ideas with real merit. This is the creative method used by advertising and marketing people. You can do it, too. Many products have been saved from the very threshold of extinction with this method. A famous baking soda manufacturer might long ago have gone under if it had hoped to continue selling to women who baked their own bread. Housewives still buy the product; they have been reeducated to its value as a laundry "sweetener," a carpet cleaner, a refrigerator deodorizer.

But you needn't wait for the threat of possible extinction to use this creative method. You can begin today, this minute.

LESSON NO. 95:
THE "WHO ELSE" CLOSE

Who Else Should Know about This?

Who else will participate in the final decision? Who else will use this? No matter what the prospect told you initially, *always* ask these questions when it comes time to close. Some closes seem to take an interminably long time for the simple reason that there are several "layers" of buying authority that you don't even know about. For example, you may have been calling on a department head who has authority to buy up to certain limits and from certain preapproved suppliers. But he or she doesn't tell you this. Unless there is common-sense evidence to the contrary, you should assume that something like this is happening in every protracted sales/closing situation. Protect yourself against loss of your precious time by asking: Who else will use this? Who else should know about this? Who else will participate in the final decision?

Who Else Should You Ask to Verify Information You Have?

You can only close if you are talking to the right person. Who else can corroborate what you have learned? Some large firms have such lax security that you can walk into the plant and talk to anybody you want to. Just because some person seems to be in charge and is willing to listen, that doesn't mean that he or she has real authority to initiate a first-time order or, for that matter, to buy at all. Discreet inquiry by telephone can save embarrassment for your contact and frustration for you.

Who Else Needs This?

Once you have closed your first deal in a new customer's facility, you have confirmation that you have been talking to the right party. Or do you? Is the person you sold the *only* one who can use your product? In some large organizations there are several possible buyers. Your present contact may or may not know who they are. If you can get the names of more possible customers from your contact, by all means do that. However, don't be put off if your contact pleads ignorance. You may yet uncover additional users through your own diligence. Every time you call on your contact, keep your eyes open. Get to know as many other people as you can. Ask other people you meet this same question: "Who else might be able to use my product?" Closing your second and third prospects in the same facility is usually just a matter of telling your new contacts: "You have authority to buy this; your firm is already using it in other departments."

Who Else on the Outside Needs This?

Engineers, department heads, supervisors sometimes know others of the same rank working in other firms. Ask about this, and ask for referrals to these people. Some of your contacts will even be willing to make a phone call for you. This kind of referral, especially if it is for a staple product which can be ordered as existing supplies are used up, is often as good as a sale.

LESSON NO. 96:
WHERE ELSE AND WHEN ELSE

Closing with Other Locations

Once you have established a relationship with one branch of a large concern, it is often just a matter of meeting the people in the other locations. But you have to know about them first. Since it is not uncommon for branches and affiliates to go by different names, be sure to ask, "Where else does your company have branches?" You may have to ask somebody besides your contact, maybe the front office. Once you have learned where these locations are, you must learn who the people are. It may surprise you to learn that even highly placed employees sometimes don't know who their counterparts are in various branch offices and plants. However, if you develop a strong relationship and a good reputation for quality service, you will find that your customers are willing—often eager—to help you get started in the other branches. And a start under these conditions can be as good as a close.

The "When Else" or "Future" Close

This close depends for its effectiveness on the natural proclivity most of us have for putting things off. This close works because it seems to let the buyer off the hook. You lead into this close by using "future-date" questions. Here's how it works. Suppose you have tried to close several times, and your prospect balks. You say something like, "I know that you feel you should not buy this now. When would be a better time for you?"

Your prospect may answer with something like, "Oh, I don't know. See me after the first of the year." Of course, you know by now that this is not an order. It's not even a commitment, and it's certainly not a close. It's a put-off. However, there is still something in the prospect's statement that can sometimes be salvaged—converted into a sale. It all depends on how you handle it.

You look at your calendar thoughtfully. "Let's see, that will be about eight weeks from now. I won't be in this part of the territory then . . . Tell you what, though. I will be making deliveries through here again in about three months. Can you wait until then?" The answer is almost certain to be "yes." You need to move quickly to convert this into a real sale. Pull out your orderbook and say out loud, "That will be on March 3" (or whatever). Then write the date where it goes in the orderbook. "And which color do you want us to hold for you—the grey or the beige?"

Obviously, this will not always work. But if it works even *once,* you'll close a sale you would surely have lost otherwise. It does work, however—often enough to make it well worth the effort of using it.

Pulling the Date Back to the Present

A curious thing about the "Future Close" is that once you get it on paper and get it signed (yes! they will sign it), it seems at once to change in character from a "maybe" to a sure thing. A prospect may feel right up until the moment of signing the order that this was something he or she was going to do later on. Once the order is signed everything changes. You may even call it a "memorandum order" or anything else you like. The prospect may realize that she can cancel the order at any time before she actually takes possession of the merchandise (certainly she knows this), yet she has quit putting it off and has *acted.* Perhaps this is why the next move works as often as it does. Here's what you say next:

"I may be through here earlier than I anticipate. Perhaps as early as three weeks or so. If I am through here then, is it okay if I just bring your unit on over?"

In well over half the cases, the prospect will say, "Oh, go ahead and bring it any time."

The buying decision is sometimes made in one leap. But at other times it is made in slow, painful steps, with the prospect kicking and screaming all the way. Sometimes what happens seems totally logical. More often, however, it is not.

LESSON NO. 97:
THE CLOSED-BRIEFCASE GAMBIT

Closing on Your Way Out

This close works so well perhaps because it is so unexpected. It seems impromptu, spontaneous. It's as though you've just thought of something important that you forgot to mention during your presentation. You have seemingly accepted the fact that you are not going to make this sale, have closed your briefcase, and are just about to leave. Then you "remember" just a couple more points.

By now you have realized that although I have listed and described several closing techniques in this chapter, most of these "closes" are intended to be used in tandem with several other closes. The "closed briefcase" is no exception. The points which you have "just remembered" could be, say, the points that you have learned for your Blast-of-Heat close (Lesson No. 88), or the Blockbuster (89), depending on which of these closes you have already used and which are still available for you to use.

Whatever you decide to use in the Closed-Briefcase Gambit, be sure that you get right into it. You'll want to do this right as the prospect begins to relax, but before he or she turns to something else.

Carry Something in Your Pocket

Since you have put all of your props away, you will need to keep something in your pocket or purse that you can flash to recapture your client's attention. He or she is likely expecting a business card or brochure at this point, so quickly explain exactly what this new prop is. If you fail to do this, you may find your new exhibit plopped into a file before you can do anything about it, while the prospect says, "I'll call you when I need something." To keep control, say as you hand over your exhibit, "Here's something I forgot to mention." Briefly describe what the exhibit is about, and go into the close you have selected, tying it in with the exhibit.

Forgetting Your Briefcase

If you have nerves of steel and you still haven't used all your ammunition, you can lay your briefcase down while making this last-ditch presentation, then walk out and leave the briefcase. You will, of course, "remember" it before you leave the vicinity of the building. When you go back in for it, thank your prospect again for the interview, and use one of your remaining closes as described in this chapter.

Perhaps I have given you the impression that you are to keep hammering away at a prospect, even when he or she shows no interest in your proposition. That's not at all what I am suggesting. What I am suggesting is that as long as there is the slightest show of interest, as long as you can actually hold the prospect's attention with your presentation, you should keep trying to sell and to close. I do not—emphatically NOT—mean that you should keep talking and trying to close while your prospect has your elbow and is trying to usher you out the door.

There is no closing strategy clever enough or strong enough to close a sale for a product that hasn't first been *sold*. But really *learn* these closing techniques and more of your sales wind up where they count—in your orderbook and in your commission check.

LESSON NO. 98: ASK

Just Ask for the Business

I once knew an office-supply salesman in Lake Charles, Louisiana who prided himself on his "simplicity." He called himself a "plain old country boy from Elton [a small town nearby] trying to get by in the big city." He used just one approach and just one close, and, in his "simple" way, did both at the same time. Here is the way he opened, and here is the way he closed:

"I'm a nice guy. I sell office supplies at a reasonable price, and whatever you order today, I deliver tomorrow. Buy something from me."

This close is certainly not going to work if you sell battleships, trucks, industrial equipment, or mutual funds, is it? Sometimes. Of course, I don't mean that you could walk into an oil refinery and say, "I'm a nice guy. I sell process-control computers at a reasonable price, and what you order from me today I deliver next month. Buy something from me." Simplicity is a lot more complicated than that.

When There's No Time for a Presentation

Perhaps you've made an appointment to see a prospective client. You've called to confirm your appointment, and everything is okay. But as you approach your target's office, the door opens and she walks briskly out the door. "Sorry," she says, "something came up at the last minute. I have to catch a plane."

What do you do? First of all, you show your understanding. "I'll see your secretary and book another appointment. Have a nice trip," you say as you walk alongside her. Maybe you ask where she is going. A lot depends on the kind of relationship you have had up until now. What about just asking for her business? Sure! What can you lose? Your chances for success may be nil if this is your first call on a complex proposition, but if you have laid quite a bit of groundwork there is absolutely no reason why you shouldn't try for a close even though there are still some unanswered questions. A close like this sometimes works:

"Mrs. Brown, why don't I just go ahead and install the system now? We can work out any problems much more easily with everything in place. And of course, we won't bill you until everything is working like it should."

What can you lose? She might say yes.

When There Is Time for a Presentation, Ask

Even when there is time for a complete presentation, why go through it if you don't have to? My wife, Bonnie, had for years wanted a well-known set of encyclopedias. One day she decided she was going to buy it and called the Houston sales office, which sent a representative out. She told the rep that she had long wanted his product. Yet he went through a one-hour presentation before writing the order. Perhaps this gentleman felt that he was giving better service by doing that. And you can't fault him for that. But if you could close just 5 or 10 percent of your deals just by asking for the business, you could invest the saved time in more presentations. If you have any reason at all to believe that your prospects understand what you are selling—*ask them to buy*! Ask early. On your way in, ask. Ask often. On your way out, ask again.

LESSON NO. 99:
ON KEEPING THE SALE "CLOSED"

Don't Wait for Something to Go Wrong

You haven't really closed a sale if it goes sour after you leave. Keeping your client sold on you and on your product means service after the sale. And good service means good record keeping. Many salespeople have the idea that service means taking care of complaints right away. You'll want to do that, of course, but many customers *don't* complain when something is wrong—they just quit buying. A thoughtful review of guarantee obligations, servicing data, etc., is made much easier by careful record keeping. Such record keeping enables you to stay on top of things; to catch things that are wrong with your product or service before your client does. However, there is a kind of "service failure" that may never surface as a complaint. A client might ask you to do something that you are not strictly obligated to do, but which could easily lead to additional sales at some time in the future. In the press of day-to-day obligations to other customers, you could easily overlook this request. You learn that this is a mistake when a customer tells you, "I asked you to check on such and such. When you didn't, I gave the business to somebody else who was able to do it for me."

Cross-Filing Makes Retrieval Easy

A filing system that requires you to remember exactly where you put things is next to useless. The system that is described here is one that will enable you to keep up not only with the *names* of your clients but with their needs and wants as well. If all you had to worry about was how to find a client in your file when somebody gave you the name, you really wouldn't need much of a file, the phone book would work as well. Suppose, however, that you have just learned of a new device that doubles the productive capacity of one particular type of machine you have been selling. You'd want all of your customers who had bought that machine to know about the new device. With a straight alphabetical filing system you would need a prodigious memory, or you would have to look through your entire file for the names of customers who had bought the machine in question.

The "Everything" File

The filing system suggested here is one in which you can file every kind of information you will want to retrieve later. Yet it is small and compact enough so that you can carry it with you wherever you go; it will fit into an attaché case. To begin with, you will need a loose-leaf binder, ruled paper, and a set of A-to-Z index tabs. Here's the way you use these items as part of a "system." When you make an entry in your "everything" file, begin by writing a "locator number" first. For example, suppose that the first entry has to do with a request from a regular customer that you help him find a new "logo" idea, which he could use to improve the appearance of his next printing order. Your entry might be something like: "101 11/22/97 Johnson Motor Company. Fred Johnson plans to change his letterheads. Wants ideas that could give his printing a new look, yet still get across what he sells." Now turn to the back of your loose-leaf binder. At "J" you will have several ruled sheets. On one line you will write "Johnson Motor Company, #101." That's all. Then turn to "L" in your index, where you will have more ruled sheets. On one like you will write "Logo #101." Of course, every time you call on Johnson you'll check his file to see what's there. But suppose that three months from now, after Fred Johnson's logo request has gotten cold in your memory, you run across a "logo" idea in a book of graphic-art designs. If you remember Fred Johnson's name in connection with this, that's fine; you can just look up his address or phone number and contact him. But if you *don't* remember his name, you simply look up "logo." Either way, you are referred back to the same locator number—#101! This is a simplified explanation, but you will readily perceive that you can have as many cross-reference points as you need to be sure that you will never again forget or overlook a client's request.

LESSON NO. 100:
SEVEN KEYS
TO HARMONY AND HAPPINESS
IN BUSINESS RELATIONSHIPS

1. *Wisdom.* Great knowledge is not necessary for the possession of wisdom. Wisdom comes from a certain internal "processing" of knowledge. This processing permits one to see relationships and connections that those who are only knowledgeable fail to see. Wisdom enables one to find *meanings* where others see only facts.

2. *Skill.* If you are granted a long life, you will undoubtedly learn to do several, perhaps many, things well. However, there should be *one thing* that you do extremely well. Life's chances may bring this one thing to you, or you may deliberately seek to develop this skill. Success, harmony, and happiness come more surely to the person who early finds the thing he so well likes doing that he would do it *free,* and then *learn to do it so well that others will be willing to pay money to have it done.*

3. *Confidence.* Do everything you do with a feeling of absolute assurance that you are the *best person* to do the thing *at this time.* If the job must be done *now* (and haven't you found that most jobs must be done now?), don't concern yourself over who might be better for the job *later.* Enter into every new task only after first reminding yourself that you are the one person best suited to do the job in this place and at this time. Do this no matter what the task is, and soon you will be rewarded with that delicious flush of confidence that comes automatically with knowing that you can bring the task to fruition.

4. *Equanimity.* While you will want to approach every task with confidence, you must remember that it is optimum *performance* that you are confident of. You *believe* in the results, of course, but you don't feel *responsible for* these results. You are responsible only for your actions. There may be other factors impinging on the outcome—things unknown to you and over which you exercise no control. Never lose your absolute assurance of the ultimate outcome, but be peaceful, calm, and understanding of the *immediate results*.

5. *Integrity*. The "morality" of a bygone era sought to establish honesty and fair dealing between people by appealing to religious sentiments—or to fear of punishment, here or hereafter! A person of integrity is one who has learned the truth about the "golden rule." This truth is that *as you do unto others, it is being done unto you*.

6. *Empathy*. This is the ability to enter into the very consciousness of the person with whom you are interacting. When you empathize with a friend, a customer, a business associate, you think and you feel like he or she thinks and feels. To do this, you will have to put aside your own feelings in any situation in which you are involved. Then you will ask yourself, "How would I think, feel, and act if our roles were reversed?" Imagine yourself standing *inside of the other person* and looking out at you. Do this deliberately until it becomes habitual.

7. *Energy*. The old saw, "Do something—even if it's wrong," has merit when the extra ingredient, *energy* is added. With energy, you can try many possible solutions to a problem and still not give up. Edison tried more than a thousand materials in perfecting the filament for his light bulb. Build physical energy through the use of the IDEA formula: *I*magination (see yourself moving with zest and verve), *D*iet (you know when you're eating right, don't you?), *E*xercise (just a one-hour walk—or two half-hour walks—each day will do it), and *A*ction (daydreaming is fine if it results in a *plan that you put into action, NOW*).

Index

180